E. H. HARRIMAN:
Master Railroader

THE EVOLUTION OF AMERICAN BUSINESS: INDUSTRIES, INSTITUTIONS, AND ENTREPRENEURS

Albro Martin, Series Editor
Oglesby Professor of the American Heritage
Bradley University

Editorial Advisory Board

Alfred D. Chandler, Jr., Isidore Strauss Professor of Business History,
Harvard Graduate School of Business Administration

Diane Lindstrom, Associate Professor of History and Women's Studies,
University of Wisconsin, Madison

Harold C. Livesay, Professor of History,
Virginia Polytechnic Institute

Peter D. McClelland, Professor of Economics,
Cornell University

E. H. HARRIMAN:
Master Railroader

By Lloyd J. Mercer

TWAYNE PUBLISHERS · BOSTON

E. H. Harriman: Master Railroader

Lloyd J. Mercer

Copyright © 1985 by G.K. Hall & Company
All Rights Reserved
Published by Twayne Publishers
A Division of G.K. Hall & Company
70 Lincoln Street, Boston, Massachusetts 02111

First Printing

This book was designed by Marne B. Sultz
and typeset in Times Roman with Univers display type
by P&M Typesetting Inc., Waterbury, Connecticut.

Frontispiece photograph of E. H. Harriman
by Sherer, New York.

Maps reproduced from the *Traveller's Official Guide
of the Railway and Steam Navigation Lines in the
United States and Canada* (1893).

Printed on permanent/durable
acid-free paper and bound in
the United States of America

**Library of Congress
Cataloging in Publication Data**

Mercer, Lloyd J.
E.H. Harriman, master railroader.

(The Evolution of American business)
Bibliography: p. 172
Includes index.
1. Harriman, Edward Henry, 1848–1909. 2. Businessmen
—United States—Biography. 3. Capitalists and
financiers—United States—Biography. 4. Railroads—
United States—History. I. Title. II. Series.
HE2754.H2M47 1985   358'.092'4 [B]   85-8441
ISBN 0-8057-9802-1

CONTENTS

LIST OF TABLES

CHRONOLOGY

1848 E. H. Harriman born in the Episcopal rectory at Hempstead, New York.

1860–1862 Attends Trinity School, Manhattan.

1862 Starts work as office boy, then messenger clerk, for D. C. Hays, Wall Street.

1869 Managing Clerk, D. C. Hays, Wall Street.

1870 Purchases seat on New York Stock Exchange.

1874 First big success in stock market. Sold short as "Deacon" White attempted a corner on the "anthracite" stocks.

mid-1870s E. H. Harriman & Company formed.

1876 Start of Tompkins Square Boy's club.

1879 Marries Mary Williamson Averell.

1880 Elected to the board of directors of the Ogdensburg & Lake Champlain Railroad.

1881 With partners buys controlling interest in Lake Ontario Southern. Purchases bonds of Illinois Central subsidiary.

1882 Lake Ontario Southern reorganized as Sodus Bay & Southern with Harriman as vice-president.

1883 Becomes sole owner of Sodus Bay & Southern. Elected to board of directors of the Illinois Central.

1884 Sells Sodus Bay & Southern to Pennsylvania Railroad.

1885 Retires from the firm of E. H. Harriman & Company. Buys the Parrott estate, which is to become "Arden."

1887 First contest with Morgan: Dubuque & Sioux City. Elected vice-president of the Illinois Central.

1889 Conflict with E. T. Jeffrey regarding rate setting for the Illinois Central.

1890 Successfully opposes massive investment program for Illinois Central which saves it from dificulty in 1893 collapse of railroads. Resigns as vice-president of Illinois Central.

1894 Opposes reorganization plan for Erie proposal by Morgan.

1897 Joins in reorganization of Union Pacific. Becomes director and member of executive committee of the Union Pacific.

1896 Inspection tour of Union Pacific. Elected chairman of the board and chairman of the executive committee of the Union Pacific.

1899 Reconstruction of Union Pacific begins. Alaska cruise. Joins reorganization committee of the Kansas City, Pittsburgh & Gulf. With a syndicate of other investors purchases control of the Chicago & Alton Railroad.

1900 Elected chairman of the executive committee of the voting trust for the Kansas City Southern. Elected director of the Baltimore & Ohio.

1901 Union Pacific purchases controlling interest in Southern Pacific. Union Pacific attempts to purchase control of the Burlington. Union Pacific attempts to purchase control of the Northern Pacific. Harriman elected to boards of the Burlington and the Northern Pacific. Northern Securities Company formed. Southern Pacific reconstruction begins.

1902 Visits President Diaz in Mexico.

1903 Elected to the board of directors of the Erie. Illness and operation followed by trip to Europe. Intercession with Stuyvesant Fish regarding his activities with Illinois Central money and loan to Fish.

1904 Purchase of significant interest in the Sante Fe. Supreme Court rules against Northern Securities Company.

1905 Elected member of the executive committee of the Erie. Trip to Japan. Dissolution of the Northern Securities Company. Begins construction of mansion at Arden.

1906 San Francisco earthquake relief. Taming of the Colorado River. Sale of the Great Northern and Northern Pacific stock received in dissolution of the Northern Securities Company. Union Pacific purchase of stock of several railroads with profits from sale of Great Northern and Northern Pacific stock. Break with Roosevelt. Interstate Commerce Commission investigation of Harriman lines begins. Removal of Stuyvesant Fish from presidency of Illinois Central.

1908 Saves Erie from receivership. Federal government sues to force Union Pacific to sell its Southern Pacific stock.

1909 Family moves into new mansion at Arden in summer. Dies in September at Arden after return from European trip for health.

CHAPTER ONE

Introduction

Edward Henry Harriman (1848–1909) was one of the leading figures in American railroading at the turn of the twentieth century. In railroading this slight man (perhaps 5′4″ and 130 pounds) was truly a giant. His peak period of influence was the last twelve years of his life (1898–1909). During that period he controlled the giant systems of the Union Pacific and the Southern Pacific, as well as the smaller Chicago & Alton Railroad, and continued as a director and major force in the Illinois Central. Harriman and James J. Hill struggled for control of the Burlington, leading to formation of the Northern Securities Company, and met again in battle on the manner of divesting it of its railroad securities. Harriman also served for a time on the boards of the Baltimore & Ohio and the Erie railroads and for five years controlled the smaller Kansas City Southern. In April 1908 Harriman single-handedly saved the Erie from receivership when even the great J. P. Morgan & Company would not do so. The outcome of Harriman's genius and hard work on all these railroads was a substantial reorganization of American railroads in the midst of the Progressive Era when big business was widely viewed as "bad" and when the railroads, among the biggest of American businesses, were coming under increasing regulation. In spite of this antibusiness climate of opinion, Harriman created railroads that were larger and more powerful in their economic capability. The expanded capacity of these railroads to move people and goods, and their increased productivity, greatly benefited society. While he earned a substantial fortune for himself in these endeavors, Harriman became very popular with other owners of securities in the firms he managed because his efforts also enriched them. This book provides an in-depth analysis of Harriman's railroad finance and management career.

Harriman's popularity was not universal. The 1906 split with Theodore Roosevelt and its aftermath demonstrated the fickleness of public opinion. The behavior of Roosevelt and others reflected concern that Harriman's control of major railroad systems gave him monopoly power. Many assumed that possession of monopoly power led automatically to abuse of that power. In addition, a number of observers believed that some of Harriman's financial activities produced results adverse to the public welfare. The Union Pacific engaged in massive stock purchases in the battle for control of the Burlington. Later purchases of the stock of several major railroads were financed by the profits from the resale of the Northern Pacific and Great Northern stock acquired in the Burlington struggle and the divestiture of the Northern Securities Company's railroad stocks. This was viewed as an improper undertaking for a railroad by no less a railroad expert than Stuart Daggett.

The financial manipulations involved in the case of the Chicago & Alton were also widely viewed as unfair to the investing public, if not simply dishonest. On this subject, a leading expert, William Z. Ripley, considered the Chicago & Alton financing a classic case of stock-watering. Ripley charged that the Chicago & Alton was an example of the crippling, looting, and scuttling of a well-managed and prosperous railroad by a syndicate of unscrupulous financiers of which Harriman was the leader. Concern about the monopoly issue and the Chicago & Alton financing focused the Interstate Commerce Commission investigation in 1906 on the Harriman lines. The Commission found no case for legal action at the time, but the investigation fostered an impression of misbehavior on the part of Harriman and his associates. Two years later the federal government instituted suit to force the Union Pacific to divest itself of the Southern Pacific.

Impressions of Harriman's career in railroad finance and management differ markedly. He was held in high esteem by many. Such divergent personalities as John Muir the renowned naturalist and Otto Kahn the financier published eulogies after Harriman's death. In 1912 Muir wrote about him, "Respect and admiration for his wonderful talents, and love for the greatness of his heart and service, are every day growing."[1] A year earlier Kahn wrote of Harriman's goals: "His real purpose, to which—as I said before—money-making was merely incidental, was to do big constructive things, his real sport was to pit his strength and brain against those of other men or against difficult tasks, his real reward was the consciousness of worthy accomplishment, the sense of mastery, the exercise of power."[2] Still, to many others he was a dishonest financier and monopoly capitalist who cheated investors out of their hard-earned money and extracted a monopoly rent for railroad services from the public at large. Our goal is to evaluate Harriman the railroad financier and manager by means of scientific analysis of his accomplishments rather than emotion.

Three major activities, not directly relevant to Harriman's business career and not amenable to the analysis to be employed here, must be considered in any evaluation of him because of the perspective they provide on the man and his character. These three activities are: the New York Boys' club; the Harriman Alaska expedition; and the Harriman estate, Arden.

Harriman was instrumental in the opening of the Tompkins Square Boys' Club in New York City in 1876. This resulted from his friendship with George C. Clark of the Wall Street firm of Clark, Dodge & Company. Clark and Harriman met frequently between 1870 and 1875, often at Clark's house. The influence of the Clark family led Harriman to take an interest in social betterment work on the East Side. The Boys' Club was apparently the first organization of its kind in the United States, if not the world. A similar institution for girls, the Wilson Mission School, gave Harriman the idea for organizing the Boys' Club. In the beginning the club was strictly for recreation without dues or fees and no discrimination with regard to membership. During its first decade club membership was relatively small, but by 1907 nightly admissions ran to a thousand or more, and membership to around six thousand. In 1900 the Boys' Club found it necessary to erect its own building (five stories and a basement) at a cost of $185,000, most of which was contributed personally by Harriman. By this time the club had expanded not only its membership but its activities and interests, including a summer camp on Long Island. Harriman provided continual direction and financial support to the Boys' Club between 1876 and his death in 1909. The Boys' Club was an extremely successful social betterment project that affected a significant number of people. It was an important part of Harriman's life.

His relationship with the Boys' Club is well illustrated by a quote from Superintendent Francis H. Tabor. Tabor said with regard to Harriman, "he was president of the Club for the first eleven years after I became superintendent, and during all those years he never refused anything which I considered of benefit to the boys. If I called at his office, the affairs of the Boys' Club were never once kept waiting, and thousands of the youth of the East Side would today bear witness to the help which his wise generosity has given them."[3]

Harriman's public-spirited activities were not confined to Manhattan's East Side. In the spring of 1899 his doctor recommended a long vacation. Following this advice, Harriman decided to take a summer cruise up the coast of Alaska to Kodiak Island, where D. G. Elliot of the Field Columbian Museum in Chicago had pointed out the possibility of hunting the Kodiak bear. Such a cruise in 1899 required that one supply the ship, and whatever else was required. The steamship *George W. Elder* with a crew of sixty-five officers and men was engaged for the cruise and refitted to Harriman's specifications. This provided much more space than needed by the Harriman family and the friends going with them. Harriman decided to make use of this excess capacity by providing a free trip for scientists, photographers, and artists. The scientific staff was selected in consultation with Dr. C. Hart Merriam of the United States Biological Survey. In the end, the technical staff gathered for the voyage consisted of two photographers, three artists, and twenty-five scientists. Among the latter were specialists in ornithology, zoology, geology, botany, and forestry. This staff represented three museums of natural history: the Field Columbian Museum in Chicago, the U. S. National Museum (Smithsonian) in Washington, and the Museum of the California Academy of Sciences; three agencies of the federal government: the U. S. Biological Survey, the U. S. Geological Survey, and the U. S. Department of Agriculture; and six major universities: Cornell, Yale, Harvard, Amherst College, the University of California, and the University of Washington. John Muir, the California naturalist, after some initial misgivings, joined the expedition as a guest of Harriman.

The Alaska expedition's scientific accomplishments were considerable. The discovery and exploration of the hitherto unknown Harriman Fjord in Prince William Sound and its associated Harriman Glacier was an important geographical achievement. Several previously unknown glaciers, as well as some that were only vaguely or imperfectly known, were mapped and described during the expedition. The large natural history collections made during the voyage included some six hundred new species. Twenty-two special papers based on the collections were published as "Proceedings" by the Washington Academy of Science. Thirteen illustrated volumes and eleven monographs by scientific members of the party were also published by the Academy.

The Alaska cruise was the culmination of Harriman's long-standing interest in the outdoors and outdoor activities. This interest had manifested itself earlier in hunting, fishing, and related activities in the Adirondacks and in the purchase of a great estate. In 1885 Harriman bought at auction the 7863-acre Parrott estate in the Ramapo Highlands about forty-five miles north of Jersey City and ten miles west of the Hudson River, apparently in part to save its forests from the timber buyers evident at the sale. After that Harriman bought adjoining land at every opportunity. By 1905 the purchase of about forty wooded tracts and farms had enlarged the estate to almost thirty square miles making it one of the most extensive country estates in the vicinity of New York. The Harrimans made it their permanent summer home. They gave it the name of Mrs. Parrott's family, "Arden."

The Parrott homestead was reserved in the sale to Harriman but the reservation did not include a cottage formerly occupied by a married daughter. After enlarging and improving it, the Harrimans residence at Arden was the former cottage. Construction of the Harriman mansion at Arden did not begin until 1905 and was not completed until after Harriman's death in 1909. The family could not move into the new home until the summer of 1909.

Conservation and management of the forests comprising about six-sevenths of the estate received Harriman's attention over the years. He also interested himself in the development and extension of the dairy industry in Ramapo Valley. In 1896 he organized a corporation, Arden Farms Dairy Corporation, to manage the agricultural development of the estate. A portion of the Harriman lands was given to the State of New York after his death (as he had arranged) and became Harriman Park, a part of the Hudson River park system enjoyed by hundreds of thousands of New Yorkers every year. Arden House now belongs to Columbia University and is the site of various scholarly meetings.

As we see, three of Harriman's activities—the New York Boys' Club; the Alaska Expedition; and the Harriman estate, Arden—left significant and valuable legacies to following generations. In the overall picture of Harriman the man, these are important considerations in addition to his activities as railroad financier and manager. Harriman's business career left as its monument rebuilt and reorganized railroads that improved the efficiency of the railroad transportation system of the United States. Our detailed attention is focused on Harriman's business career, but his non-business activities provide an insight into Harriman's character that is often overlooked.

We turn next to a sketch of Harriman's business career from an office boy at age fourteen to chief executive of the greatest railroad system in the United States if not the world. Following this we will examine in more detail each of Harriman's major railroad endeavors. This examination will embrace separate chapters on the Harriman involvement with the Illinois Central and the Southern Pacific, and two chapters on the management and financial aspects of Harriman's control of the Union Pacific. The latter will include the struggle for control of the Burlington and the Northern Securities case as well as the Union Pacific's substantial financial activities following settlement of the case. Because of the great controversy surrounding it, a separate chapter will be given to the Chicago & Alton. Another chapter will deal with the relatively smaller involvement with the Baltimore & Ohio, the Erie, and the Kansas City Southern. One chapter is an essay on what we can learn from Harriman's career for business and business management in the 1980s. The final chapter is a bibliographical essay.

A major focus in evaluation of Harriman's activities in railroad finance and management is assessment of his impact on the efficiency of the railroads with which he was associated. One major tool for this evaluation will be estimates of the rate of return on the capital in railroads that Harriman managed. Estimates of both the usual accounting rates of return and the internal (economic) rate of return will be prepared for this purpose. Where possible, rates of return in the Harriman period will be compared to similar estimates for the period preceding his management and control.

A second important tool to evaluate the change (if any) in efficiency and productivity with Harriman management will be an examination of indexes of physical productivity for the Harriman railroads. Wherever possible, this will include a comparison of the Harriman period with the preceding period. Comparison of physical productivity for the Harriman railroads with contemporary physical productivity for the United States rail system as a whole is also provided.

Our second major focus is the evaluation of Harriman as railroad financier. Here we are concerned with the efficiency of his financial activities. What was the impact of these activities? Did they weaken (as some have charged) the railroads involved? Did he really engage in "stock-watering''? Did the investing public lose as a result of Harriman's manipulations?

The management and financial focus of this investigation provides a basis for some firm conclusions on the impact of Harriman's activities on the railroad system and its ability to serve the public. Such analysis provides a far better basis for understanding the man and his contributions (and seeing what they have to say for our own time) than the partial stories and myths put forward by past detractors and glorifiers.

CHAPTER TWO

The Harriman Business Career

Edward Henry Harriman began his education in the public schools of Jersey City. After a few years his father, the Reverend Orlando Harriman, decided that something better was required and sent Henry and his three brothers to Trinity School in New York City. Clergymen's sons could attend Trinity School for only a small charge. The Reverend Harriman had himself been a prize-winning scholar at Columbia University and placed a high value on education. Harriman's mother, Cornelia Harriman, formerly Cornelia Neilson, was a member of an old and distinguished New Jersey family. She believed her children were superior to their surroundings, including the immigrant children in the Jersey City schools. Harriman thus had ample parental push to better himself through education.

One of the drawbacks of attending Trinity School was the necessity to walk from the ferry to the school—a route that led to encounters with the rough street boys of Manhattan's West Side. Young Henry, slight though he was, proved in this situation that he could take care of himself. This was one of the things that toughened him for the struggles of his later career.

Harriman attended Trinity School for two years. While not a scholar in the mold of his father, he acquired knowledge rapidly and with great facility. In his last term at Trinity he won the first prize for scholarship.

Harriman's toughness and single-mindedness is illustrated by the fact that, as a boy of fourteen, he one day marched into his father's study and announced, "Father, I have become convinced there is something else in life besides school and books. I am going to work.'' His parents resisted what they believed to be youthful impetuousness, but in the end the boy's stubborn insistence carried the day.

Thus it was that Harriman left school in 1862 to become an office boy in the stock exchange house of D. C. Hays for five dollars a week. This was as much or more than Orlando Harriman earned after twenty years in the ministry. John Moody, the famous financial writer, says that Harriman's job in 1862 as an office boy for DeWitt C. Hays on Wall Street was obtained by his father. Other writers don't actually say who got him the job, but it seems probable that his older brother, who already worked on Wall Street, had something to do with it. Given the unworldliness of Orlando Harriman and his initial opposition to Edward's going to work, Moody's account appears implausible.

In his early business career a good part of Harriman's earnings went to his family. He soon moved from office boy to messenger clerk (''pad-shover'') which provided an education in the rudiments of finance and monetary affairs. In this day, before ticker quotations, it was the messengers who broadcast prices and offers to buy and sell by running between brokers on Wall Street and its environs. In this job Harriman showed powerful perception and an accurate and retentive memory. This experience combined with his own talent and capacity for work provided the basis for his advancement in the business world so that in 1868 or 1869 he became the managing clerk in Hays's office. These first years on Wall Street provided Harriman with a solid education in the intricacies of the world of finance.

In the summer of 1870 Harriman at the age of twenty-two bought a seat on the New York Stock Exchange with a $3,000 loan from his uncle, Oliver Harriman, who was a wealthy merchant. One apocryphal story says that Harriman made enough money on Black Friday of 1869, when Jay Gould's attempt to establish a corner on gold collapsed, to buy the exchange seat. With his seat on the stock exchange, Harriman was successful both as a broker working on commission and with his own stock speculation. In the mid-1870s he gave his friend James B. Livingston an interest in the business, and the firm name became E. H. Harriman & Company.

In his first three or four years as a broker Harriman confined himself primarily to the commission business. He showed himself to be not only shrewd, but careful, even tight, with his money. At this time a broker received a two-dollar commission for a 100-share transaction. Generally when a broker went to lunch he gave unfilled orders to another to execute. The other broker than retained the commission. Harriman did not follow this practice. He executed all orders in hand before going to lunch. No two-dollar commissions easily escaped his grasp. Gradually he accumulated capital. His first big success came in 1874. He received a profit of $150,000 by selling short as "Deacon" White attempted to corner the "anthracite stocks." White failed in his effort and the value of the stocks plummeted. A little later Harriman demonstrated that no one is right all the time as he took a short position in Delaware & Hudson stock. Unfortunately for him, a much wealthier man, John Jacob Astor, happened at the same time to decide to buy all the Delaware & Hudson stock he could get. Consequently the price rose steadily until the short-sellers were obliged to cover at a substantial loss. Much of Harriman's anthracite stocks profit was lost in this transaction. His commission business remained profitable and in the long run his speculative gains outran losses.

During his first years as a stockbroker, Harriman developed working relationships and friendships with a number of young men prominent on Wall Street and in the social circles of New York. Included in this group were August Belmont, Jr., Stuyvesant Fish, William Bayard Cutting, R. Fulton Cutting, James B. Livingston, Dr. E. L. Trudeau, and George C. Clark. Several of these men played important roles in his later career.

Harriman did not spend all his time at work. He was a director of the Traveler's Club and a member also of the Union and Racquet Clubs. Another activity was participation in the National Guard. As a child, one of Harriman's favorite pastimes was playing with his toy soldiers. In fact, he dreamed of becoming a soldier and accomplishing great things. He was too young for the Civil War although he had been chosen as captain of a group of older boys who marched along with Union soldiers on their way to war in the early days of the war. In his first years on Wall Street Harriman belonged to the Seventh Regiment of the National Guard which had the reputation of being the best militia organization in the state of New York. He drilled with August Belmont, Jr. and other Wall Street associates and is reported to have become an expert marksman. He was early attracted to the Adirondacks for outdoor activities including fishing and hunting. Boxing and trotting horses were other avocations. The latter became his primary hobby in later years.

Over his career Harriman was very successful in his stock market investments. He became one of the dominant figures on Wall Street. No less a financial expert than Bernard Baruch, who also started with nothing, wrote of Harriman, "He was the man I did my best to emulate when

I first entered Wall Street.'' Baruch also wrote that Harriman seemed to him ''. . . to be the epitome of all that was dashing.''[1]

Harriman's entrance into the field of railroad management came in 1880 when he became a director on the board of the Ogdensburg & Lake Champlain Railroad Company of which his new father-in-law, William J. Averell, was president. Harriman married Mary Williamson Averell in 1879 in Ogdensburg. The directorship in his father-in-law's railroad and the experience gained in it turned Harriman's attention to railroads as a business and investment vehicle. In the fall of 1881 he and some partners bought the controlling interest in a small and unprofitable railroad, the Lake Ontario Southern.

The Lake Ontario Southern was a reorganization of the Ontario and Southern which had begun business in the early 1870s. The road was thirty-four miles in length running from the town of Stanley to a harbor on Lake Ontario known as Great Sodus Bay. The road connected with the Pennsylvania Railroad at Stanley and the New York Central at Newark. It is said that the physical condition and equipment of the road were poor and that it was generally regarded as an unprofitable and undesirable property. What Harriman apparently saw in the road was the strategic position provided by its location and connections with the Pennsylvania Railroad and the New York Central.

In 1882 the Lake Ontario Southern was reorganized as the Sodus Bay & Southern with S. J. Macy as president and Harriman as vice-president. Following the reorganization, improvements in the physical condition of the road and additions to its equipment were begun. To encourage grain traffic, the Sodus Bay Elevator Company was formed in 1882 and a grain elevator erected at Sodus Bay. Despite these changes, operation of the road continued to be unprofitable.

At a board of directors meeting in October 1883 Harriman named a price at which he would either sell his stock or buy that of the other owners. As a result, Harriman became almost the sole owner of the property. The board was then reorganized with Harriman as president.

Improvements in physical condition and equipment were continued, and in the spring of 1884 Harriman offered the road for sale to both the Pennsylvania and the New York Central. In this maneuver he exploited the location of the road and the competition between the Pennsylvania and the New York Central. To the Pennsylvania he argued the desirability of an extension to Sodus Bay, thereby obtaining an outlet on Lake Ontario for the coal of the Pennsylvania fields. With the New York Central Harriman's argument was that the Pennsylvania would surely buy the road if the Central did not and that the latter should keep its rival from obtaining the road even if the Central did not particularly need it. He argued that Great Sodus Bay was the best harbor on the south shore of Lake Ontario and the railroad that controlled it would have a major advantage over competitors for the increasing trade with Canada.

The New York Central took an option on the road until noon on 1 July. A few days after the New York Central undertook the option, the Pennsylvania expressed a desire to buy the road. At the last moment the New York Central decided to renew the option, but Harriman was absent from his office until after the option expired and the Sodus Bay & Southern was sold to the Pennsylvania.

This first excursion into railroad finance and management was apparently quite profitable for Harriman. It showed his careful exploitation of two conditions, a strategy to which he would return frequently in his later career. First, a railroad's capital equipment had to be in good physical condition. Second, location and strategic position in the market was perceived as a valuable asset and one that could be exploited for capital gains.

Career in Railroad Finance and Management

In the 1870s one of the oldest and most successful railroads in the United States, the Illinois Central, began a new policy of extension of its lines in response to rising competition from an increasing number of east-west lines which reached into its territory. A rising force in the director-ate of the Illinois Central at this time was Stuyvesant Fish, member of a wealthy New York family and the son of President Grant's ex-Secretary of State. Fish had a long-standing friendship with E. H. Harriman. Fish had also been a director of the Ogdensburg & Lake Champlain. One result of his ascendancy at the Illinois Central and his friendship with Harriman was the direction of Harriman's interest toward the Illinois Central. This interest first manifested itself in 1881 in the purchase of bonds of one of the Illinois Central's subsidiary roads, the Chicago, St. Louis & New Orleans, which was the Illinois Central's vehicle for extension down the Mississippi Valley.

The combined influence of the firm that had placed Illinois Central stock in Holland and which held the proxies for that stock (the Boissevain Brothers) and of Stuyvesant Fish, who had become vice-president of the Illinois Central, led to the election of Harriman as a director of the Illinois Central in May 1883. On the board of directors his influence was exerted in support of a bold policy of improvement and expansion. He became closely associated with Fish in the management of the road. The Illinois Central increased its mileage about a thousand miles in the first five years after Harriman became a director. The directorship of the Illinois Central marks the significant reorientation of Harriman's career toward railroad finance and management. While he also remained active in the stock market, he retired from the firm of E. H. Harriman & Company in 1885.

In 1886 Harriman for the first time battled J. P. Morgan for control of a railroad. The object of their interest was the Dubuque & Sioux City, then leased by the Illinois Central. Continued profitable operation of the Dubuque & Sioux City road required a significant investment by the Illinois Central that would only be worthwhile if the Illinois Central owned the road rather than leased it. As the result of some adroit legal maneuvering by Harriman concerning the voting of proxies held by Drexel, Morgan & Company, a board favorable to the Illinois Central purchase was elected at the Dubuque & Sioux City annual meeting in early 1887. Litigation over the matter continued for some months and ended with the acceptance by Drexel, Morgan & Company of a compromise offer by the Illinois Central. Soon after this victory, Harriman was elected vice-president of the Illinois Central in place of Stuyvesant Fish who had moved up to the office of president.

As vice-president and chairman of the finance committee of the board of directors Harriman had a profound influence on the management of the Illinois Central over the next few years. It was in these years that his ability as a railroad manager was sharpened and he learned the practical, physical side of the transportation business. These lessons provided the working basis for his crowning achievements with the Union Pacific and the Southern Pacific in later years. On behalf of the Illinois Central Harriman pushed for the purchase of the leased lines in Iowa and their linkage to the main line. He also led the way to purchase of the Louisville, New Orleans & Texas with its extensive mileage and import terminals in Memphis and New Orleans. During Harriman's first decade with the Illinois Central the railroad added 1,500 miles, 234 new passenger cars, 274 new locomotives and 8,401 new freight cars. Gross annual earnings more than doubled from $8.9 million to $20 million. Harriman continued as a director and leader of the Illinois Central through the remainder of his life.

His greatest achievement was the reorganization and rebuilding of the Union Pacific Railroad. The Union Pacific Railroad had been placed in the hands of receivers in October 1893. The original reorganization committee struggled for two years to find an acceptable plan to revive the railroad. In the late fall of 1895 the reorganization effort was placed in the hands of Kuhn, Loeb & Company with Jacob H. Schiff leading the way. The reorganization plan developed by Schiff's committee ran into opposition at all points. Upon investigation, Schiff discovered that the opposition was led by Harriman who stated to Schiff that his purpose was to reorganize the Union Pacific himself. Harriman's original intention appears to have been to unite the Illinois Central and the Union Pacific. His opposition to the Schiff plan was based on the fear that it would give control of the Union Pacific to the New York Central and Chicago & Northwestern with the Illinois Central shut out. Harriman's price was chairmanship of the executive committee of the reorganized road. He used Illinois Central credit to carry the day against Schiff. With the sound credit of the Illinois Central Harriman could obtain the funds necessary for the Union Pacific reorganization at 3 or 3½ percent versus the 4 to 5 percent Kuhn, Loeb would have to pay to obtain the same funds. Schiff eventually proposed a compromise that Harriman accepted. If Harriman worked with rather than against the reorganization committee he would be made a director of the reorganized company and a member of the executive committee. Harriman agreed and became a director and member of the executive committee in December 1897. Harriman and Schiff's collaboration paid handsome dividends to both since Harriman soon became chairman of the board of directors of the Union Pacific and Kuhn, Loeb & Company became the primary bankers for the reorganized railroad.

Harriman brought not only his own genius, but tremendous financial resources to the Union Pacific. Added to the substantial funds of Kuhn, Loeb & Company were those of the New York City Bank and its president James Stillman. In addition, from his stock market years and the Illinois Central, Harriman had connections with the Goulds and Vanderbilts. In 1902 William Rockefeller and Henry Rogers of Standard Oil, and in 1904 H. C. Frick of U. S. Steel, joined the financial combination built by Harriman. These tremendous financial resources were necessary because the reorganization required $58 million to be paid in cash. Altogether about $75 million had to be raised.

The key to the Union Pacific reorganization was the agreement on repayment of the Union Pacific's debt and accumulated interest to the government. Various attempts had been made in Congress and in negotiations with the government to refund the debt and accumulated interest. These efforts failed. Reorganization was accomplished when the committee agreed to pay the government debt, both principal and interest, in full and in cash. The reorganization plan was a strong one which considerably reduced fixed charges and laid the substantial foundation on which Harriman later built during his control of the Union Pacific.

Under his management the Union Pacific engaged in both financial maneuvers and a substantial physical restructuring. Both efforts paid off handsomely. The financial operations of the Union Pacific in the Harriman period divided into three parts. The first involved regaining control of the principal auxiliary systems. Second was acquisition of control of the Southern Pacific through purchase of large amounts of stock and the attempt to share in control of the Burlington (this involved the purchase of Northern Pacific stock and the formation of the Northern Securities Company). Third was the very profitable sale of the stock acquired in the fight over the Burlington and the use of the proceeds for purchase of Chicago & Alton, Atchison, Topeka & Santa Fe, Baltimore & Ohio, Illinois Central, and other stocks.

Harriman's greatest achievement was in the physical restructuring and operation of the Union Pacific. Over $50 million was invested in betterments and new equipment by 1904. About $15 million of this was financed from operating income. Between 1898 and 1907 the average capacity of the railroad's freight cars was raised from 20 to 34 tons. In 1898 the average Union Pacific locomotive weighed 37 tons. This increased to 68 tons in 1909. Freight and passengers carried by the railroad increased about fourfold between 1899 and 1907. Thus, as Daggett points out, "From the point of view of operation the success of the Union Pacific has been remarkable."[2]

Besides creating the potential for greatly increased revenue, the Harriman rebuilding also reduced costs relative to revenue. The result was a substantial rise in profits. In 1907 total fixed charges of the Union Pacific were $8.6 million while net income was $45 million. Ten years before the road had been in receivership because of its inability to pay its fixed charges. In 1907 dividend payments were $23.5 million and $10.6 million was added to surplus.

While the rebuilding of the Union Pacific was getting underway in 1899, Harriman was asked to serve on the reorganization committee for the Kansas City, Pittsburgh & Gulf, a 778-mile railroad running from Kansas City to Port Arthur on the Gulf of Mexico. The railroad, which had gone into receivership in April 1899, had been constructed in sections over the period 1888–1897. The quality of the construction was apparently poor, and the railroad was not well managed prior to the receivership.

When the road was reorganized in April 1900 as the Kansas City Southern, the stockholders assigned all their power to a voting trust of which Harriman was a leading member. He was selected as a member of the executive committee and its chairman. He served in the position with the Kansas City Southern for the five-year duration of the voting trust.

Under the Harriman management, gross earnings of the road rose from $3.6 million to $6.5 million while net earnings increased from $0.9 to $1.9 million. During the five years $5.5 million were spent on improvements, additions, and new equipment.

After the end of the voting trust Harriman's management of the Kansas City Southern was attacked by the new managers in their first annual report after taking over the road. The new managers ascribed the road's difficulties to neglect of maintenance. This charge was accepted by later writers. Based on the annual report cited, Edward S. Mead mentions the Kansas City Southern as an extreme illustration of the evils of neglected maintenance. William Z. Ripley adds his criticism on this point, stating that the stockholders in recovering their property from the voting trust on its expiration ''discovered that it was almost completely gutted.'' Ripley's statement is offset by another statement he makes that the ''Kansas City, Pittsburgh and Gulf in 1900 (after the reorganization) was physically rebuilt and also structurally solidified throughout.''[3] Obviously both statements cannot be correct and we will examine this point in more detail later.

In 1899 Harriman along with a syndicate of other investors purchased control of the Chicago & Alton Railroad. The Chicago & Alton was an apparently prosperous but conservatively (one can argue poorly) managed railroad. It had paid dividends of 8 percent on its invested capital for thirty years or more and its stock was selling at seventy-five to one hundred points above par value. With respect to these statistics, the Chicago & Alton could not have differed more from the Kansas City Southern. In another way, the Chicago & Alton was very much like the Kansas City Southern. Mead states that the Chicago & Alton had not kept its property up to standard. Its conservative management had not spent enough to provide the extensions, betterments, replacements, and additional equipment necessary to serve a rapidly developing territory. The road had aged without improving its physical condition. Annual earnings in the eleven years before 1898 had declined by $2.7 million. In 1898 a group of large stockholders approached Harriman with the idea of reorganizing the company's finances. Harriman had S. M. Felton, a well-known expert and railroad manager, make a thorough examination of the property. With Felton's report, Harriman was satisfied that the Chicago & Alton could be bought for less than its potential value and he formed a syndicate to buy the company.

Harriman's control of the Chicago & Alton involved considerable physical improvement of the road with $22.3 million being spent on permanent improvements during the Harriman management. Gross earnings rose from $6.3 million in 1898 to $12.8 million in 1907 (Harriman's last year with the Chicago & Alton) and net earnings from $2.7 million to $4.4 million. At first glance this seems like evidence of a good job of management. Yet the Harriman control of the Chicago & Alton was a major focus of the Interstate Commerce Commission investigation of 1906 and is the source of considerable controversy and charges against Harriman. The reason for this lies in the financial manipulations of the Harriman syndicate which are briefly outlined here and considered in more detail below.

The syndicate initially acquired 97 percent of the stock of the Chicago & Alton. A total of $32 million of new three-percent bonds were offered to the stockholders at sixty-five soon after the reorganization. The new directors then declared a cash dividend of 30 percent on the stock of the Chicago & Alton ($6.7 million). In 1900 the Chicago & Alton Railway Company was formed as a holding company. The holding company sold its stockholders $22 million of 3.5 percent collateral trust bonds at sixty. The old preferred stock of the Chicago & Alton was purchased with the proceeds of this sale and, in exchange for $18.3 million of old common stock of the Chicago & Alton, the holding company issued $19.5 million of its own common and $19.5 million of its own preferred stock. The holding and operating companies were consolidated in 1906, the small outside holdings of the original railroad stocks being taken up by issuance of "prior lien and participating" stock.

The substantial increase in the nominal capitalization of the Chicago & Alton by the activities noted (about $54 in bonds and $39 million in stock) with only about $25 million in betterments and extensions ($22.3 in betterments and $3 million for purchase of the St. Louis, Peoria & Northern Railway) has been the cause of severe criticism of Harriman's control of the railroad. Also of concern was the fact that fixed payments were due on about $12 million in 1899 and $70 million in 1907. On the surface, this whole episode contrasts rather sharply with the rest of Harriman's career in railroad management and finance and will be given detailed analysis in a later chapter.

In his reconstruction of the Union Pacific, Harriman was faced with one serious obstacle to significant improvement of the efficiency of the system. That obstacle was the Central Pacific Railroad between Ogden and Sacramento. The gain from the significant increase in the carrying capacity of the Union Pacific's Ogden-to-Omaha line would not be fully realized if the capacity of the Central Pacific's Ogden-to-Sacramento line remained unchanged. The Southern Pacific (which owned the Central Pacific) rebuffed repeated attempts by Harriman to buy the Central Pacific. The death of Collis P. Huntington in August 1900 opened the door for Harriman to get the Central Pacific by attaining control of the Southern Pacific.

Early in 1901 Harriman obtained from the Union Pacific board of directors the authorization for issuance of $100 million of 4 percent, first-mortgage convertible bonds of the Union Pacific. The Union Pacific began buying Southern Pacific stock soon after Huntington's death. By 31 March 1901 a total of 275,000 shares had been purchased and 475,000 shares transferred to the Union Pacific from Edwin Hawley and the Huntington estate at a cost of about $42 million. Altogether these shares represented 38 percent of the outstanding stock of the Southern Pacific Company. Another 150,000 shares of common and 180,000 shares of preferred were soon added giving the Union Pacific 45.5 percent of the outstanding shares and effective control of the Southern Pacific.

Reconstruction of the Central Pacific was soon begun and completed in three years. This rebuilding involved abandonment of 373 miles of old road and substitution of 322 miles of new track, substantially reducing curves and grades. The most remarkable portion of this new road was the Lucin cutoff across the Great Salt Lake. A comparable engineering achievement on the main line was the Bay Shore cutoff which tremendously improved the entrance into San Francisco. The reconstruction of the Central Pacific cost about $18 million while over the same period more than $20 million was spent on betterments for the rest of the Southern Pacific. This included a third major cutoff, the sixty-mile Montalvo cutoff on the main line between Burbank and Montalvo in Southern California. The three main cutoffs cost about $20 million out of the almost $30 million spent on betterments with another $41 million spent on new equipment.

The implicit merger of the Union Pacific and the Southern Pacific was widely regarded as detrimental to society because of the increased monopoly power of the combined lines. The Interstate Commerce Commission argued that the Union Pacific's control over the Southern Pacific "effected a substantial elimination of competition between the two lines." One of the main recommendations of the ICC in its study of the Harriman lines was that, given the policy of maintaining competition between naturally competing lines, "the ownership of any stock by one railway in a competing railway should not be permitted, and such lines of railway should be prohibited from having any common directors or officers."

In our later evaluation of Harriman's management of the Southern Pacific it will be instructive to evaluate the question of reduced competition (growth of monopoly power) with regard to the Southern Pacific. Our overview here suggests considerable improvement of the efficiency of the Southern Pacific and consequently also the Union Pacific as a result of Harriman's management. Society surely benefited from this improvement. The issue is whether there was an offsetting or larger negative impact produced by reduced competition between the Southern Pacific and the Union Pacific.

In 1905 Harriman turned his attention from the United States to a larger stage, the world. His interest was attracted to the Orient by Kuhn, Loeb & Company's floating of Japanese war bonds and his own connection with the Pacific Mail Steamship company. Lloyd C. Griscom, the American ambassador to Japan, invited Harriman to visit Japan in the spring of 1905. Harriman accepted this invitation out of his curiosity to see the Orient and because he had a vision of an around-the-world transportation line. This globe-belting line would include the Pacific mail steamships from America to Japan and Port Arthur; the railroad across Manchuria, China, and Russia to a Baltic port; and steamship to New York.

The railroad portion of Harriman's vision included the South Manchuria Railroad, the Chinese Eastern, and trackage rights on the Trans-Siberian Railway to the Baltic Sea. This grand plan failed in part because of popular reaction in Japan against Americans due to President Roosevelt's role in negotiations for the peace treaty to end the war with Russia. The Japanese public felt that they had won the war, but everything was given away by the peace treaty. The transfer of the South Manchuria Railroad to Japan required the consent of China by one article of the peace treaty. Such consent was not forthcoming. The opposition of Baron Komura, Japanese Minister of Foreign Affairs, to American influence provided the final blow to Harriman's plans. Komura succeeded in convincing his colleagues to break off negotiations with Harriman. Jacob Schiff of Kuhn, Loeb & Company visited Japan in 1906 and attempted to revive the negotiations. Again Komura carried the day.

Natural calamities in 1906 led to significant demonstrations of generosity and resourcefulness by Harriman. The first of these was the San Francisco earthquake and fire in April 1906. Harriman learned of the disaster the day after the earthquake (Thursday, 19 April) and immediately ordered the general managers of the Union Pacific and the Southern Pacific to make the full resources of the two roads available to assist in disaster relief. Harriman himself started for San Francisco by a special train. The Southern Pacific, including its San Francisco Bay ferryboats, evacuated thousands of refugees from San Francisco and rushed hundreds of tons of foodstuffs and supplies to the city. The railroad's hospital at Fourteenth and Mission Streets was thrown open to the injured. Harriman arrived early Sunday morning and attended a conference of city leaders organized to deal with the emergency. In the month after the disaster the Union Pacific and the Southern Pacific brought over 1,600 carloads of supplies into the city and moved almost a quarter of a million people out of the city. This was accomplished with no charge by the railroads. *Railway World* in an editorial of 3 September 1909 said of Harriman's efforts, "It was primarily due to his organizing genius and energy that San Francisco so quickly rallied from its great disaster."

The second catastrophe Harriman faced in 1906 was the runaway Colorado River in California's Imperial Valley. Irrigation projects had opened the valley to agriculture and settlement within only the previous six years. Even in this short time the silt load carried by the Colorado had clogged the earliest canals. A new intake from the river was cut by the irrigation company in late 1904 to eliminate the clogged portion of the canal and let water directly into the unobstructed canal. An unexpected winter flood in 1905 enlarged the cut beyond the capability of the irrigation company to slow the inflow. Attempts to correct the problem in the summer of 1905 failed.

The irrigation company, the California Development Company, then found itself in financial difficulty and applied to Julius Kruttschnitt, general manager of the Southern Pacific, for a loan on the grounds that financial assistance was warranted because of the traffic the Imperial Valley was providing the railroad. He turned the request down, but the company petitioned Harriman. After an investigation and report, Harriman consented to a $200,000 loan against the advice of Kruttschnitt and others. In hopes of improving the management of the development company, the Southern Pacific as a condition of the loan stipulated the right to select three directors, one of whom would become president of the company. Also 51 percent of the company's stock was to be placed in the hands of a trustee as collateral security for the loan. The Southern Pacific's aim in these arrangements was to see that its loan was wisely spent and repaid. It had no intention of taking over ownership of the California Development Company.

A second tremendous flood occurred in November 1905. Virtually the entire river then poured into the valley creating a large new lake in the Salton Sink. By June 1906 the Colorado was discharging six billion cubic feet of water every day into the Salton Sea which was rising seven inches per day over a four-hundred-square-mile area. The main line of the Southern Pacific was inundated and in the course of the summer of 1906 the tracks were moved to higher ground five times.

By June 1906 the fight against the runaway Colorado River was entirely in the hands of the Southern Pacific Railroad. With immense effort, high rock-fill dams were built which closed the crevasse created by the river through the new 1904 intake. This was completed in early November. Unfortunately a new flood in December broke a reconstructed earthen levee of the California Development Company and in three days the entire river once again rushed to the Salton Sea. The only solution was to close the new crevasse with rock-fill dams and to build a stronger levee along the west bank of the river for at least twenty miles.

Up to this point the Southern Pacific had spent about $1.5 million on controlling the Colorado. The railroad's annual freight revenue from the Imperial Valley at the time was at most $30,000. Permanent control of the Colorado was estimated to cost an additional $1.5 million.

Since the Southern Pacific's interests in the Imperial Valley were small compared to the nation's, Harriman requested federal help of President Roosevelt in December 1906. Roosevelt urged Harriman to go ahead, pleading that Congress was adjourning for the holidays. Harriman showed his generosity and public spirit by having the Southern Pacific complete the work. The total cost to the Southern Pacific was about $3.1 million.

Presidents Roosevelt and Taft both sent bills to Congress to partially reimburse the Southern Pacific for its efforts and expense. In 1911 a proposed appropriation of $1,663,000 having been reduced to $773,000 was finally reported favorably by committee to the House. Opposition of five representatives, who described the bill as "an attempted raid on the federal treasury," resulted in no action being taken on the bill by the House. In the end the Southern Pacific received neither reimbursement nor even thanks from Congress. Harriman on his own initiative, and with his stockholders' money, saved a valuable resource, the agricultural wealth of the Imperial Valley, for the nation. The nation gave him the back of its hand in return.

Harriman had relatively minor involvements with three other railroads in his career: the Baltimore & Ohio, the Erie, and the Santa Fe. The connection with the Baltimore & Ohio lasted eighteen months between 1899 and 1901. He was a director of the Baltimore & Ohio over this period and was credited by its then general manager Frederick Douglass Underwood with playing an important role in raising $32 million needed for improvements and new equipment in the reorganized road.

When Mr. Underwood was elected president of the Erie in 1901, Harriman expressed interest in becoming a director of that railroad. In September 1903 Harriman was elected to fill a vacancy on the board of the Erie and a short time later became a member of the executive committee. In this position he was instrumental in 1905 in obtaining the financing to build two extensions designed to improve grades, etc., which then became subsidiary roads to the Erie. The two railroads were the Erie & Jersey and the Genesee River. These two branch lines significantly reduced grades in their divisions, reducing operating costs, and increased the carrying capacity of the railroad. Harriman remained on the Erie board until 1906. He constantly pushed for new equipment and betterments during his tenure. The improvement in financial strength and operating efficiency of the Erie certainly owed something to his presence and the application of his motto that "the way to save money is to spend it."[4] By this he didn't mean that money should be squandered, but that expenditures that increased the earning capacity of the railroad should be undertaken.

Harriman's greatest service to the Erie came in 1908. The Erie had $5.5 million in short-term notes maturing on 8 April 1908. When J. P. Morgan & Company and others refused to cover this obligation, Harriman saved the Erie from receivership by personally making the loan against the advice of his friends. This action considerably enhanced his reputation.

Harriman's involvement with the Santa Fe was occasioned by the fact that the Santa Fe and the Southern Pacific were competing lines and that in the period 1902–1904 both railroads set out to build on the low-grade route through Gila Cañon in Arizona. By a narrow margin (20 minutes) the Southern Pacific's proxy, the Arizona Eastern, first filed the required location maps to obtain right-of-way on public land through Gila Cañon. In the ensuing litigation the Arizona Eastern's right-of-way through Gila Cañon was sustained over that of the Santa Fe's proxy, the Phoenix & Eastern Railroad Company. The case was appealed to the Supreme Court by the Santa Fe; however, before a decision was rendered, a compromise was reached by which the Southern Pacific bought at cost the capital stock of the Phoenix & Eastern.

While the Gila Cañon contest was under way in the summer of 1904, Harriman and some other associates purchased 300,000 shares of Santa Fe stock giving them two directors on the Santa Fe board. Harriman himself did not take a directorship on the Santa Fe board. H. H. Rogers and H. C. Frick were elected to represent the Union Pacific and the Southern Pacific interests.

In the last years of his life Harriman concentrated his attention on the Union Pacific and the Southern Pacific. The federal government in early 1908 brought suit in United States Circuit Court to separate ownership of these two railroads on the grounds that the joint ownership was a combination in restraint of trade under the Sherman Act. The case was not decided in Harriman's lifetime and while the first decision was in favor of the Union Pacific, the appeal to the Supreme Court resulted in an order for the Union Pacific to dispose of its control of the Southern Pacific. While this legal action was underway, the Southern Pacific under Harriman's direction pushed extensions into Mexico and completed about 800 miles by mid-1909. Altogether about $114.5 million was spent on construction or purchase of new lines and branches by the Southern Pacific during Harriman's control. In 1909 about 40 percent of railroad investment in the United States was undertaken by the Union Pacific and the Southern Pacific. Thus, while Harriman was frequently ill in his last years, he was not idle. He stayed in the thick of action until his untimely death 9 September 1909.

Harriman was a devoted family man. His relationship with his wife, Mary, was very close. His estate of around $70 million was left entirely to Mary with a simple will of only about eighty words.

To society, Harriman left a legacy of rebuilt and refinanced railroad systems. These were profitable to their owners and their improved efficiency was advantageous to the traveling and shipping public. He also left substantial controversy regarding some of his financial deals and the effect of his "empire" on competition in railroad transportation. We turn now to a detailed examination and evaluation of these issues.

CHAPTER THREE

Learning the Business:
The Illinois Central, 1883–1909

Harriman learned the railroad business during a long tenure with the Illinois Central Railroad Company beginning with his election to that firm's board in May 1883. The operating and financial experience he gained with the Illinois Central provided the basis of knowledge and experience for his great works between 1897 and 1909. Before undertaking these, he served an apprenticeship of about fourteen years with the Illinois Central.

On paper the Illinois Central got its start almost half a century before Harriman became associated with it. The settlers of Illinois in the early 1830s were eager to use the new invention of overland transportation, the railroad, to solve their transportation problems. The promoters of one major project, the Central Railroad Company, obtained a charter through a bill passed in December 1835 by the Illinois legislature. These promoters envisioned their railroad as part of a national system and argued that it would provide benefits far beyond the border of Illinois. In 1836 a bill was introduced in Congress to provide right-of-way to the Central Railroad through public lands in Illinois along with the privilege of purchasing adjacent land. The basis for this proposed subsidy to the Central Railroad was the argument that the railroad was not solely a local project, but one of national significance. The Central Railroad was seen as the main stem of a rail transportation system which would extend from the Old Northwest to the South and Southeast.

The act incorporating the Central Railroad provided that it and other contemplated railroads would be administered by a board of commissioners. This board was created and the commissioners began work on the Central Railroad in 1836. Grading for the Central Railroad was begun at Cairo, Galena, and intermediate points, and by 1840 about one million dollars had been spent on surveys and construction. Lack of funds led to suspension of the work in 1840. All that remained of this work when the Illinois Central Railroad Company was incorporated in 1851 was forty miles of poorly constructed and useless embankment extending north from Cairo. Illinois's grand scheme for internal improvement left it with the embankment cited, one locomotive, twenty-four miles of poorly constructed railroad using wooden ties capped with iron straps, and a large public debt not paid off for over a decade.

Early in 1848 both Sidney Breese and Stephen A. Douglas introduced bills in the Senate with significantly different provisions to aid a railroad in Illinois. Douglas sought a direct grant of federal lands to the state of Illinois while Breese's bill called for direct aid to the private corporation. Douglas wanted the railroad to run not only from Cairo to Galena, but also to Chicago. Douglas's bill passed by a wide margin in the Senate, but lost by fourteen votes in the House. The bill was reintroduced in the next session of Congress with an amendment introduced by Senator King of Alabama extending the land grant to Alabama and Mississippi in connection with a proposed railroad from Mobile to the Ohio River. Following long debate the bill passed the Senate on 3 May 1850 and the House on 17 September. Thus did the Illinois Central become the first land grant railroad.

A group of investors (a collection of Eastern capitalists) was the winner in the contest to control the land grant and the railroad. Morris Ketchum, founder and head of a banking house and a locomotive manufacturing firm, was the leading member of the winning group. Associated with Ketchum were thirteen others including Robert Schuyler, president of the New York & New Haven and three other railroads. At this early time Schuyler, like Harriman half a century later, was viewed as the "Railroad King." Ketchum's thirteen associates were the incorporators of the new railroad, named the Illinois Central Railroad Company, and these, along with Governor Augustus C. French of Illinois as an ex-officio member, became the first board of directors. The bill providing the charter for the Illinois Central was signed 10 February 1851. One of many unique features in the Illinois Central charter was the requirement that in lieu of other taxes the railroad would pay the state 5 percent of gross operating revenues of the land-grant lines in the state of

Illinois plus a state tax bringing the total on these lines to 7 percent. The state debt totaling over $16.6 million at the time was eventually paid off by the proceeds of this tax.

As with all pioneer railroads, raising the capital for construction of the Illinois Central was a difficult undertaking. The first effort in England in the fall of 1851 was unsuccessful. Money only began to flow in significant amounts after $4 million in bonds were taken by the incorporators themselves and various Eastern banking houses. This was accomplished by February 1852. Charles Devaux & Company of London then sold another $5 million in bonds by 1 August. After this, British iron manufacturers were willing to accept the bonds at par for rails and other iron. Construction was pushed ahead vigorously and the road opened to Dubuque, Iowa on 11 June 1855. The entire road (705.5 miles) was completed to Cairo on 27 September 1856. The Illinois Central was then the longest railroad in the United States, being about double the length of the Erie.

The financial panic and economic downturn of 1857 almost pushed the railroad into insolvency (its floating debt was then about $3.8 million), but it was assigned on behalf of the creditors to a special committee of assignees with George B. McClellan as chairman. The committee with the aid of various American and English financiers pulled the road out of the crisis so that by the spring of 1859 the board of directors authorized the resumption of dividend payments and started an unbroken string of dividend payments that was to contiue for seventy-two years (until 1931).

The Illinois Central expansion beyond its original line began a decade after its completion with the 1 October 1867 leasing of the Dubuque & Sioux City Railroad. The Dubuque & Sioux City itself had a 40-year lease commencing 1 January 1867 on the Cedar Falls & Minnesota Railroad. The Illinois Central assumed this lease for twenty years. The Iowa Falls & Sioux City Railroad was organized 1 October 1867 to build the remaining 183.8 miles of the old Dubuque & Sioux City and also leased for forty years to the Illinois Central. By the end of 1870 the Illinois Central was operating 1,107 miles of railroad, an increase of 60 percent in mileage in only three years.

The main push by the Illinois Central during the 1870s was to establish a connection to New Orleans and the Gulf of Mexico. In 1872 the Illinois Central entered into a contract with the New Orleans, Jackson, & Great Northern Railroad and the Mississippi Central Railroad to construct a connecting link for a through line from Cairo to New Orleans and to interchange traffic. Under the contract the Illinois Central was to invest one-eighth of its earnings in the consolidated mortgage bonds of the two railroads up to $150,000 per year for ten years. In 1873 this was modified to $200,000 per year to a total of $5 million. With this agreement the southern lines were able to sell enough of their bonds to improve their roads and extend the Mississippi Central from Jackson, Tennessee, to Filmore, Kentucky, about four miles from Cairo. The through line was opened on 24 December 1873.

The two southern roads were merged the following year under the title of the New Orleans, St. Louis & Chicago Railroad. In 1874 $5 million gold 7 percent bonds of the southern roads were exchanged for $1 million of Illinois Central 5 percent bonds. The New Orleans, St. Louis & Chicago defaulted on interest due on consolidated mortgage bonds of its constituent companies in 1876 and went into receivership on 10 March. The Illinois Central instituted foreclosure and the New Orleans, Jackson and Great Northern was foreclosed 17 March 1877 and reorganized as the New Orleans, Jackson & Great Northern Railroad on 12 May. The Mississippi Central was foreclosed 23 August 1877 and reorganized as the Mississippi Central Railroad on 5 November. On the latter date the two roads were again consolidated as the Chicago, St. Louis & New Orleans. The management of that railroad was assigned to an Illinois Central vice-president (Stuyvesant Fish) on 1 January 1878. Formal consolidation with the Illinois Central did not occur until 1 January 1883.

About 130 miles of branch line was added to the Illinois Central between 1878 and 1882. Other than this, investment by the Illinois Central was quite low in the 1870s and early 1880s. Current dollar investment expenditure between 1871 and 1882 appears to have *totaled* only about $6 million compared to an *average* of $5.2 million per year between 1896 and 1909 when Harriman's influence was at its peak.

The Early Harriman Years

The momentous personnel change of the 1870s for the Illinois Central was the election in 1877 of thirty-two-year-old Stuyvesant Fish to the board of directors. Fish was the son of Hamilton Fish, Secretary of State in the cabinet of President Grant. In addition to serving on the Illinois Central board, Fish was first treasurer and agent of the purchasing committee of the New Orleans, Jackson & Great Northern Railroad and then vice-president of the Chicago, St. Louis & New Orleans Railroad between 1877 and 1882. He earned a strong reputation as a railroad financier in these positions and on 7 January 1883 was elected vice-president in charge of financial affairs in New York for the Illinois Central.

A long-standing friend of Fish was E. H. Harriman. That friendship and Fish's connection with the Illinois Central were probably important factors in Harriman's initial interest in the Illinois Central. Harriman took a large block of Chicago, St. Louis & New Orleans bonds from Fish in 1881 and about this time began to buy Illinois Central stock which was somewhat in disfavor on Wall Street. By early 1883 Harriman appears to have determined to get a foothold in the Illinois Central by becoming a member of its board. The influence of Fish and the Boissevain Brothers firm, which voted the proxies for Dutch shareholders, was sufficient to get the thirty-five-year-old Harriman elected to the Illinois Central board on 30 May 1883 in place of A. G. Dulman who had represented the Dutch shareholders of the Illinois Central for a number of years.

According to his biographer, Harriman's influence on the Illinois Central board was, from the first, exerted in support of a bold policy of improvement and expansion. It is certainly the case that the sixties and seventies had seen a relatively low level of investment and expansion at the Illinois Central. The first stirrings of change were evidenced by the thrust southward with the acquisition of the Chicago, St. Louis & New Orleans. The quarter century after 1883 was to see enormous change at the Illinois Central. There seems littledoubt that Harriman was a prime mover in the "new" Illinois Central.

During Harriman's first year on the board the Illinois Central operated two thousand miles of railroad, 80 percent more mileage than it had operated through most of the seventies. By 1909 operated mileage was up to 4,547, more than four times the seventies level and more than double the level when Harriman came on the board. Gross operating revenue grew more than fourfold (from $12.2 million to $53.7 million: the peak was $56.6 million in 1907) during Harriman's tenure. Capital earnings (gross operating revenue minus operating expenses and taxes) increased threefold in the same period: from $5.5 million in 1884 to a peak of $16.5 million in 1907. Another way of viewing this is that for the Illinois Central capital earnings grew from $5.4 million in 1890 (by which time Harriman was definitely a dominant power at the Illinois Central) to $13 million in 1907, an increase of 141 percent. This was a period of rapidly expanding business for all railroads in the United States. However, for all U. S. roads as shown in *Historical Statistics of the United States* the increase in capital earnings was only 115 percent over the years 1890–1907. The same disparity shows up in the growth of gross operating rev-

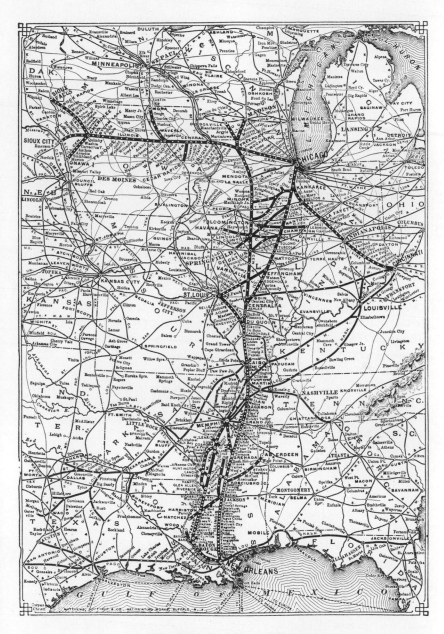

1. The Illinois Central System

enue, that of the Illinois Central expanding 227 percent between 1890 and 1909 while all U. S. roads grew but 135 percent. The Illinois Central was among the leading performers of U. S. railroads while Harriman was active in its management.

Shortly after Harriman joined the Illinois Central board (15 August 1883), James C. Clarke became president. With increasing competition from other trunk lines, it had become obvious that the Illinois Central needed more branch and feeder lines. Clarke, strongly supported by Fish and Harriman, initiated an aggressive expansion program in 1886–1888. This new policy included several steps: (a) construction from Chicago to Freeport, Illinois, along with branches to Madison and Dodgeville, Wisconsin; (b) acquisition of the Havana, Rantoul & Eastern between LeRoy, Illinois, and Lebanon, Indiana; (c) acquisition of the Illinois branch of the Champaign, Havana & Western from Champaign to Havana and White Heath to Decatur; (d) construction of a branch from Manchester to Cedar Rapids, Iowa; and (e) construction of branch lines from Cherokee, Iowa, to Onawa, Iowa, and to Sioux Falls, South Dakota. The value of new and acquired capital in this three-year period was about $15 million, almost three times the total for the decade of the seventies. In the first six years that Harriman was on the board the Illinois Central increased its mileage almost nine hundred miles (about 50 percent).

Harriman's central role in this period is shown by his presidency in 1888 and 1889 of the Rantoul Railroad Company organized 3 June 1887 as a subsidiary of the Illinois Central, and his role in gaining control (at bargain prices) of what became the Chicago, Havana & Western Railroad Company organized (October 1886) in the interest of the Illinois Central and formally leased by that company in March 1888.

In the summer of 1885 Harriman retired from his brokerage firm and turned his primary attention to railroading. His Wall Street experience was undoubtedly valuable to Harriman in this new field of endeavor. He was a great manager and rebuilder of railroads, but he also became a recognized leader among railroad financiers. In the sixties and seventies railroad bonds in the United States typically carried coupon rates of 6 or 7 percent. Just as typically these bonds were not generally sold at par by the railroad. Sales around 65 were not uncommon. The result of this is that the railroads paid 10 percent for their borrowed money, not 6 or 7 percent. The Illinois Central with its strong, established finances and revenue base (in part the outcome of the land grant subsidy) was a leader in breaking this financing pattern. It sold the first 6, 5, 4½, and 4 percent railroad bonds in the United States. In the early 1880s Stuyvesant Fish carried out the first sale (at par) of 3½ percent bonds for the Illinois Central. Harriman followed this lead and improved on it, selling (at par) 3 percent bonds by the middle nineties. Thus, he obtained funds at one-third the cost of a decade or two earlier. Interest rates had declined greatly over this period, but Harriman still sold bonds at a significantly lower interest rate than the average in the market. This kind of financial wizardry was what he meant when he sometimes said, "I think this is a good time to buy some money."[1]

One of his first major accomplishments with the Illinois Central led him into his initial skirmish with J. P. Morgan with whom he was to do battle on several occasions in his later career. The need for expanded feeder lines was increasingly clear as the eighties wore on. A major feeder of the Illinois Central was the Dubuque & Sioux City which the Illinois Central was operating under lease and for which the Illinois Central was paying 38 percent of gross revenue. In 1884 the Dubuque & Sioux City began to operate at a loss. The solution to the shortfall was expansion of the feeders to the Dubuque & Sioux City. Such expansion would be at the expense of the Illinois Central and, given the conditions of the lease, would primarily benefit the lessor. The Dubuque & Sioux City lease was to expire 1 October 1887. Harriman brought before the Illinois Central board the proposal to purchase the Dubuque & Sioux City and was authorized to do so either by private negotiation or by purchase of stock in the open market.

The majority stockholders of the Dubuque & Sioux City decided to take advantage of this situation by forcing the Illinois Central to buy their stock at par or to initiate a new lease providing them guaranteed dividends at 4 percent per year. Their ploy to bring this about was to give their stock to Drexel, Morgan & Company as trustees and invite other shareholders to join them. By late 1886 Drexel, Morgan & Company held a majority of the Dubuque & Sioux City stock. Harriman had obtained about fifteen thousand shares in the market (Drexel, Morgan & Company held almost thirty-three thousand shares), but this was insufficient for control and no more stock was to be found at a reasonable price.

Despite the apparent control of Drexel, Morgan & Company, the next annual meeting (14 February 1887) found Illinois Central interests controlling a majority of those stockholders actually present. The Illinois Central interests organized the meeting and nominated five directors (a majority) of their own. During the vote a large number of shares voted by proxy were rejected by the meeting on the grounds that proxy voting in Iowa (the meeting was held at Dubuque) was not legal. Moreover, the entire block held by Drexel, Morgan & Company was rejected also on the grounds that the vote had been signed by Drexel, Morgan & Company personally rather than as trustees. The only shares allowed to vote were those held by Harriman. A board majority representing the Illinois Central was elected.

This matter led to litigation that continued for some months. Morgan refused to compromise and insisted on the original terms: purchase of their shares at par or a new lease with 4 percent dividends guaranteed. By authority of the Illinois Central board, Harriman finally made an offer of 80 for the Morgan shares. This offer was accepted by Morgan and the Dubuque & Sioux City became the property of the Illinois Central on 1 October 1887.

Early in 1887 Fish succeeded Clarke as president of the Illinois Central. Harriman's position and importance in the Illinois Central had also expanded along with his demonstrated skills in management and finance. As a result, he was elected vice-president of the Illinois Central on 28 September 1887.

Harriman's first major conflict with a high official of the Illinois Central occurred in the summer of 1889 when he was acting president while Fish was in Europe. Rate making for railroads at the time was generally at the discretion of the general manager or traffic manager. The Illinois Central in April 1889 amended one of its bylaws to reduce this discretion by making rate reductions contingent on the approval of the president who was to report his decision in such cases to the board of directors. The general manager of the Illinois Central at the time was E. T. Jeffrey, a respected and able railroad executive. Jeffrey did not agree with the bylaw change and Fish had promised him that if he remained with the road he would not be deprived of his rate-making power. In a conversation with Jeffrey in early September Harriman reminded him that, in accordance with the changed bylaw, rate reduction decisions needed to be referred to the president for final approval. Jeffrey objected strongly to this position and resigned the same day. This put Harriman in a difficult position since he was fairly new as an officer of the company and not widely regarded at the time as an experienced railroad man. Nevertheless, he stuck to the principle involved (that bylaws voted by the board should be followed by the company's officers) and appointed C. A. Beck as general manager, also moving A. W. Sullivan to general superintendent and E. G. Russell to superintendent of the Illinois lines. Harriman's actions were apparently approved by the board of directors and Fish when he returned from Europe. This incident, painful as it may have been, increased Harriman's standing and power at the Illinois Central.

While the Illinois Central was rebuilding its southern connection (Cairo to New Orleans) during 1878–1882 it was also pushing the extension of feeder lines in cotton country. The Yazoo & Mississippi Valley Railroad Company was incorporated in 1882 to tap the fertile Yazoo Delta of Mississippi. Initially the road was built from Jackson, the state capital, to Yazoo. Fish became president and Harriman vice-president of the new railroad upon its completion. An 88-mile branch was started in 1883 from Kosciusko, Mississippi, to Aberdeen, Mississippi, and opened 1 August 1884. The Yazoo & Mississippi Valley road was extended northward to Parsons in 1886, and the West & East Railroad built from Durant to Lexington, Mississippi, in 1882 was extended thirteen miles westward in 1866 to a junction with the former road at Tehula, Mississippi.

Trouble for the Illinois Central in this period developed from the efforts of Collis P. Huntington of the Southern Pacific Company to create a true transcontinental road with eastern connections from New Orleans where his western roads terminated. The completion of the Louisville, New Orleans & Texas Railroad in 1884 created the first major rival for New Orleans traffic for the Illinois Central. The Huntington interests also gained control of the Mississippi & Tennessee Railroad at about this time. This road ran from Memphis to a junction with the Illinois Central at Grenada, Mississippi. The Mississippi Central and the Mississippi & Tennessee had always complemented each other and exchanged traffic freely. When the Louisville, New Orleans & Texas railroad opened, its president informed the Illinois Central that the Mississippi & Tennessee would no longer exchange traffic with the Illinois Central when such traffic could move advantageously over the Louisville, New Orleans & Texas.

The Illinois Central's response to this pronouncement was to survey a rail route from Greenwood to the Mississippi River and north to Memphis. Whether this survey was in earnest or a bluff isn't known. It was soon followed by the result desired by the Illinois Central. The Huntington interests changed their strategy and sought an agreement with the Illinois Central allowing Harriman to buy a controlling interest in the Mississippi & Tennessee on behalf of the Illinois Central. The road came under Illinois Central control with Harriman as president in 1886, and the Illinois Central started operation of the road as a part of the Memphis division in 1888.

In the early 1890s Huntington appears to have abandoned his goal of a complete transcontinental railroad. At this time the territory served by the Louisville, New Orleans & Texas Railroad was still largely undeveloped and the railroad was struggling to pay its funded debt with nothing left for dividends. Huntington decided to sell the property, and the Illinois Central in the persons of Fish and Harriman was definitely interested in acquiring it. Negotiations began early in 1892 and on 17 June 1892 the Illinois Central purchased the Louisville, New Orleans & Texas for $5 million cash and $20 million in bonds backed by the Illinois Central. The purchased railroad was 807 miles in length with 101 locomotives, 65 passenger cars, and 2,735 freight cars. It owned large tracts of land in the Yazoo Delta and shop facilities at Memphis, Vicksburg, and New Orleans. Because it was such an important transaction, the board of the Illinois Central submitted it to the stockholders for consideration and vote. A substantial majority favored the acquisition although some major European stockholders were opposed. In October 1892 the Louisville, New Orleans & Texas was consolidated with the Yazoo & Mississippi Valley under the name of the latter road. The acquisition was not fully incorporated in the Illinois Central's accounts until 1898.

The acquisition of the Louisville, New Orleans & Texas, in which Harriman played an important role, was one of the most important extensions of the Illinois Central at that time. With this acquisition the mileage controlled by the Illinois Central had almost doubled since Harriman joined the board (in nine years). Strategically it was a major action because it removed the major rival to the Illinois Central in its southern territory. Physically it was valuable because it provided the equivalent of a double-track railroad between Memphis and New Orleans, gave the Illinois Central additional terminal facilities in those cities, and expanded the southern feeder-line network.

With the Louisville, New Orleans & Texas, the Illinois Central had a southern section complete with feeders that nicely balanced its northern (midwest) roads. Still it lacked something for completeness. That was strength in its mid-section comparable to that of the north and south portions of the developing system. The problem facing the Illinois Central is illustrated by its traffic exchanges at Memphis. Northbound traffic generated in Louisiana and Mississippi arrived in Memphis via the Yazoo & Mississippi Valley. It then had to be routed over a competing railroad or sent 100 miles south to Grenada to get on the northbound main line of the Illinois Central. This latter routing obviously left a lot to be desired.

Harriman's basic policy in a situation of this nature was to acquire railroads already built or under construction. Such a move satisfied two objectives at once. It both provided the requisite facilities and rather neatly removed competitors. During the Wall Street panic of 1893 prices of railway securities declined sharply. Taking advantage of this circumstance, Fish and Harriman in 1893 began negotiations to obtain Huntington's interest in the Chesapeake, Ohio & Southwestern Railroad between Louisville and Memphis as well as several branch lines in Kentucky and Tennessee. The Illinois Central obtained an interest in the Chesapeake, Ohio & Southwestern and then entered into a contract with the Louisville & Nashville Railroad Company to sell that interest to the latter. The consummation of this agreement was blocked by Kentucky state authorities on the grounds that the Louisville & Nashville could not legally acquire the Chesapeake, Ohio & Southwestern. In late 1894 and early 1895 the Illinois Central bought over $6 million of the bonds of the Chesapeake, Ohio & Southwestern. At about the same time the second mortgage of the company was foreclosed and the property was sold under foreclosure on 25 July 1896 to Harriman on behalf of the Illinois Central. To provide for the loan to purchase the bonds cited and to improve lakefront property to Chicago the Illinois Central shareholders voted an increase of $60 million in capital stock on 26 November 1895. As with other properties it took over, and pursuant to the policy followed by Harriman throughout his career, the Illinois Central in the years after its acquisition spent a considerable sum for improvement of the Chesapeake, Ohio & Southwestern and its affiliated lines.

At the time Fish and Harriman were obtaining the Huntington lines in Kentucky and Tennessee they were also vigorously pushing expansion north of the Ohio River. The major achievement in this second sphere was the 1 October 1895 lease of the St. Louis, Alton & Terre Haute Railroad which was comprised of eight separate railroads totaling 239 miles in length. This acquisition was an important one because (a) it extended the Illinois Central operations over its own lines to St. Louis; (b) it expanded facilities in the southern Illinois coal region; and (c) it provided a second Ohio River crossing for the Illinois Central.

Two additional important steps completed the strengthening of the Illinois Central mid-section. The first was the construction of the 131-mile line from Tara, Iowa, to Omaha, Nebraska, under the auspices of the Fort Dodge & Omaha Railroad Company. The second step was the acquisition in 1900 of the 204-mile road from Pekin, Illinois, to Evansville, Indiana (the old Peoria, Decatur & Evansville in receivership since 1894) and joint ownership in the Peoria & Pekin Union Railway. The latter was a switching and terminal railroad operating across and on both sides of the Illinois River in its namesake communities.

In 1890 Harriman had a leading role in a decision that greatly benefited the Illinois Central. The decision, contrary to his usual practice, was to go slow in spending for improvements and expansion. A special committee of the board of directors had been appointed in the summer of 1889 to prepare a report on the company's financial policy in the near future and a plan of expenditures for the next two or three years. The committee submitted its lengthy report in January 1890, strongly recommending expenditure of a substantial sum over a period of at least three-and-one-half years for improvements and expansion. The report was sent to Harriman who at the time was ill in New York. He wrote a letter giving his opinion of the report to the secretary of the Illinois Central and including the surprise statement,

I do not concur with the recommendation of the Committee on Rates, Revenues and Expenditures, and think it would be unwise at this time to pass any resolution adopting a policy for a large expenditure of money.[2]

Why Harriman chose to make such a recommendation at that time is not known. The directors of the company had come to rely on his judgment and there was little opposition to his view with the result that the proposed plan of expenditure was abandoned. For whatever reason he chose this course of action it turned out to be the right one in view of the panic of 1893 and its accompanying economic downturn. Unlike many of its brethren during this period, the Illinois Central did not face receivership, maintained its unbroken string of dividend payments, and floated its only bond issue of the period ($2.5 million in August 1895) at 3 percent.

The Later Years: Harriman in Control

Harriman was continuously active in the Illinois Central from the time he first joined the board. He was a member of the board of directors and chairman of the finance committee throughout the period. He was not continuously an officer of the company. In 1890 he resigned as vice-president so as to have more time for his burgeoning activities outside the Illinois Central. After 1890 his power at the Illinois Central rested on his position as a director and chairman of the finance committee, and on the goodwill he had built up based on the soundness of his judgment and actions. Also after 1897 his tremendous success in the railroad field beyond the Illinois Central, especially with the Union Pacific and Southern Pacific, added enormously to his prestige and influence. After 1906 the Union Pacific's ownership of a large amount of Illinois Central stock was also an important factor.

In 1906 one of the most dramatic episodes in the history of the Illinois Central unfolded as a contest developed between Harriman and Fish. The culmination of the contest was the ouster of Fish and the election of Harriman's candidate, James T. Harahan, as president of the Illinois Central.

Dissatisfaction among the members of the board of directors regarding Fish's administration had apparently been growing for some time before 1906. Both in his position as chairman of the finance committee and because he shared the feelings upon which the opposition to Fish was based, Harriman had little choice but to lead the opposition. Because of his interests with the Union Pacific and elsewhere, Harriman's motives in this affair were widely misconstrued. Many believed that Harriman simply wished to replace Fish with his own man so as to bring the Illinois Central under the domination of the Union Pacific, thereby increasing his own power. Fish and his supporters made this charge. In order to protect the credit of the company the facts of the case were not broadcast at the time.

The dissatisfaction with Fish dated from at least 1903. Upon returning from California in the spring of 1903, Harriman was informed by some other directors that Fish had deposited over $500,000 of Illinois Central money in the Trust Company of the Republic, a small and weak bank of which Fish was a trustee. There was concern about both the safety of the Illinois Central funds and the propriety of this action by Fish. Harriman had the money returned to the Illinois Central although it turned out that this could only be done in small amounts and slowly without bankrupting the Trust Company of the Republic.

In June 1903 Harriman went to Europe following an illness and operation. While he was gone, Fish again deposited a large sum of Illinois Central money in the Trust Company of the Republic. He later withdrew this sum, but a month afterwards deposited it again. Apparently his actions were intended to provide support for the Trust Company of the Republic which was having financial difficulties associated with its financing of an industrial corporation known as the United States Shipbuilding Company. Perhaps not entirely by happenstance Fish had an interest in the latter company. Also during the summer of 1903 Fish loaned himself $1.5 million of Illinois Central money with inadequate collateral security.

Following Harriman's return from Europe in the fall of 1903 several directors brought these matters to his attention and asked him to join them in deposing Fish. Harriman did not agree with this course of action and, after interceding with Fish regarding these matters, even loaned him $1.2 million to enable him to resolve his financial difficulties.

In 1904 Fish again deposited Illinois Central funds in a bank in which he was interested, the Commonwealth Trust company which was the successor to the Trust Company of the Republic. This action further exacerbated Fish's poor relationship with those Illinois Central directors who were aware of the situation. Harriman again counseled forbearance on the part of those directors.

In 1906 matters came to a head with the contest to elect a director to fill the vacancy on the board resulting from the death of William Grinell. For various reasons, including concern that Union Pacific influence was too strong on the board, Fish wanted to elect his own choice. Fish's concern may have been misguided, but it was not entirely without foundation. The Union Pacific had recently bought $28 million (par) of Illinois Central stock. Three members of the Illinois Central board were also directors of the Union Pacific. A fourth Union Pacific-related director might frequently give the Union Pacific interest a majority of those present. Fish was also undoubtedly desirous of having an ally to stand by him if there was trouble regarding his unauthorized use of Illinois Central funds.

Various skirmishes regarding proxies ensued. Finally at a meeting on 27 July an agreement was reached by which (a) the three outgoing directors would be reelected; (b) Grinell's successor would be selected by a majority of the directors; (c) the resolution calling for a new proxy committee would be withdrawn; and (d) the Harriman-Kuhn-Loeb proxies would be given to Fish.

Henry W. De Forest, a director of the Southern Pacific, was nominated on 9 October by a majority of the board (seven members) to fill the vacancy. Fish protested this selection and at the annual meeting of 17 October placed James D. W. Cutting in nomination and voted sufficient proxies to elect Cutting. At the next board meeting (November 7) Harahan was nominated for the office of president, replacing Fish, and elected with eight votes (four abstaining). Harahan had been in active charge of operations of the Illinois Central and quickly pledged no radical change in management while making it clear that the Illinois Central would not be dominated by the Union Pacific.

The Illinois Central continued its expansion in the first decade of the new century, adding another seven hundred miles of road by construction and acquisition. Substantial sums were also spent on improvements, equipment, and repair. In 1897 the Illinois Central had completed at an estimated cost of around $10 million its large Stuyvesant Docks in New Orleans. These docks, which extended at first 1600 feet, and in the end 4700 feet along the Mississippi River, were destroyed by fire in 1905 and rebuilt in 1906.

Some Results

The Illinois Central before Harriman's association with it was a prosperous and financially sound railroad. Its first major moves for expansion occurred just before Harriman joined the board. While he was associated with the Illinois Central it expanded greatly and became even more prosperous and financially secure. The continued development of the country the Illinois Central served and the upward curve of prosperity in the U. S. economy especially in the first decade of the century were important factors in the railroad's prosperity. In addition to these forces, significant credit for this success must also be attributed to Harriman. To see the change between the pre-Harriman and Harriman periods we will examine rates of return and productivity change for the Illinois Central for the periods 1870–1883 and 1884–1909.

The first rate of return examined will be the internal (economic) rate of return for the Illinois Central for the two periods. The internal rate of return, unlike accounting rates of return, is the economic rate of return on an investment project. Calculation of the internal rate of return for 1870–1883 uses the real investment and capital earnings estimates of Table 3–1. These data are in 1900 dollars with the current dollar figures converted using the Bureau of Labor Statistics Wholesale Price Index for 1890–1909 and the Warren and Pearson Wholesale Price Index for 1870–1890, the two indexes linked at 1890. Calculation of the internal rate of return for a finite time period necessitates an adjustment in the terminal year to account for the fact that the capital created by investment cost over the calculation period will continue to produce capital earnings in the future. The terminal adjustment used here is the real dollar capital stock of the terminal year calculated by the perpetual inventory method,

Table 3–1
Illinois Central
Investment Cost and Capital Earnings[a]
(1870–1909)

Year	Investment Costs (000 of 1900$)	Capital Earnings (000 of 1900$)
1870	23,350[b]	1,732
1871	258	1,720
1872	369	1,265
1873	309	1,558
1874	361	1,802
1875	318	1,852
1876	519	1,389
1877	648	1,966
1878	225	2,712
1879	326	2,906
1880	957	2,847
1881	0	3,148
1882	213	3,350
1883	1,985	4,919
1884	19,593[b]	4,856
1885	167	5,234
1886	3,578	5,402
1887	9,912	5,188

using a depreciation rate of 4 percent. The Illinois Central internal rate of return for 1870–1883 is a healthy 7.5 percent. The Illinois Central to which Harriman came in 1883 was a comfortably profitable railroad.

Table 3–1 also presents the estimated real investment cost and capital earnings of the Harriman period (1884–1909). Calculation of the internal rate of return reveals that the Illinois Central of the Harriman era was indeed a profitable railroad. For 1884–1909 the internal rate of return for the Illinois Central is 15.5 percent. This is a little more than double the profitable results of the earlier period. Economic growth and general high cyclical prosperity are a part of the difference between the two periods. Some part is also due to Harriman's management and financial genius. He learned his lessons in railroad management and finance well and applied them both here and to his other great ventures.

Another way of viewing the rate of return is the gross accounting rate of return: the ratio of capital earnings to accumulated investment expen-

Table 3–1 (cont'd)

Year	Investment Costs (000 of 1900$)	Capital Earnings (000 of 1900$)
1888	3,876	3,870
1889	4,458	4,880
1890	2,028	5,359
1891	2,625	5,146
1892	2,781	5,615
1893	3,185	6,104
1894	3,550	7,363
1895	1,552	6,676
1896	7,817	8,493
1897	8,587	7,672
1898	14,794	10,026
1899	3,611	9,196
1900	4,894	9,743
1901	5,218	11,216
1902	5,548	12,197
1903	4,622	12,201
1904	3,726	11,368
1905	4,670	13,443
1906	13,098	13,792
1907	6,839	14,238
1908	934	11,370
1909	3,759	10,772

[a]Underlying data is from the company reports in annual volumes of Poor, *Manual of Railroads.*
[b]Includes estimated capital stock.

ditures. Table 3–2 presents gross accounting rates of return for 1870–1883 and 1884–1909. The mean rate for the first period is 8.96 percent while that for the second period is 10.31 percent. The accounting rates of return show an improvement on average for the second period, but much less than that indicated by the internal rates of return. It is interesting that there is a sharp upward shift in the annual rates of return in the first period in 1878 that coincides with the beginnings of expansion of the railroad. This general higher annual rate of return is maintained throughout the second period. The decline after 1907 is related to the sharp depression of 1907–1908 in the U. S. economy and factors common to railroads in general in the United States during this period includ-

Table 3–2
Illinois Central
Gross Accounting Rates of Return
(1870–1909)

Year	Gross Capital (000 of 1900$)	Capital Earnings (000 of 1900$)	Gross Accounting Rate of Return (%)
1870	23,350	1,732	7.42
1871	23,609	1,720	7.29
1872	23,978	1,265	5.28
1873	24,287	1,558	6.41
1874	24,649	1,802	7.31
1875	24,996	1,852	7.41
1876	25,486	1,389	5.45
1877	26,133	1,966	7.52
1878	26,358	2,712	10.29
1879	26,685	2,906	10.89
1880	27,642	2,847	10.30
1881	27,642	3,148	11.39
1882	27,855	3,350	12.03
1883	29,840	4,919	16.48
		Mean rate of return	8.96
1884	30,334	4,856	16.00
1885	30,501	5,234	17.16
1886	34,080	5,402	15.85
1887	43,992	5,188	11.79

ing the increasing government regulation of railroad affairs. The maintenance of a high annual profit rate is associated in the second period with an ongoing program of improvement and expansion for the Illinois Central in which Harriman was a prime mover. The fruits of this policy are reflected in the relative rates of return for the two periods whether measured in economic or accounting terms.

Ample new and larger equipment was a prime component of Harriman's railroad management. While we cannot see directly the relative size of the equipment, we can see numbers, and the increase in numbers provides a conservative estimate of the growth of capacity in this period. Table 3–3 provides some rolling stock figures for the Illinois Central. A few earlier years are shown to give a fix on what was happening earlier

Table 3–2 (cont'd)

Year	Gross Capital (000 of 1900$)	Capital Earnings (000 of 1900$)	Gross Accounting Rate of Return (%)
1888	47,868	3,870	8.08
1889	52,327	4,880	9.33
1890	54,355	5,359	9.86
1891	56,980	5,146	9.03
1892	59,760	5,615	9.40
1893	62,945	6,104	9.70
1894	66,496	7,363	11.07
1895	68,048	6,676	9.81
1896	75,865	8,493	11.19
1897	84,452	7,672	9.03
1898	99,247	10,026	10.15
1899	102,858	9,196	8.94
1900	107,752	9,743	9.04
1901	112,970	11,216	9.93
1902	118,518	12,197	10.29
1903	123,140	12,201	9.91
1904	126,867	11,368	8.96
1905	131,537	13,443	10.22
1906	144,634	13,792	9.54
1907	151,473	14,238	9.40
1908	152,407	11,370	7.46
1909	156,166	10,772	6.90
		Mean rate of return	10.31

and annual figures for 1896–1909. Note that there is little change between 1869 and 1878 as we would expect from the investment series. In the next decade all categories of rolling stock more than doubled. The railroad's mileage also almost doubled in this period; thus capacity was not changed so much as the raw numbers of rolling stock might seem to suggest. Mileage increases about one-sixth from 1888 to 1894 while rolling stock increases in number were greater: locomotives 40 percent, passenger cars 36 percent, and freight cars 28 percent, so capacity is markedly increased in the late eighties and early nineties. This is the result that Harriman's policies were intended to produce. Capacity increases still further between 1896 and 1909. Mileage rises about one-half and passenger cars (44 percent) about match this, but the increases in

**Table 3–3
Illinois Central
Rolling Stock[a]**

Year	Locomotives	Passenger	Freight	Service
1869	177	141	4,191	n/a
1878	212	173	4,894	n/a
1888	436	388	12,474	96
1890	528	488	14,302	105
1894	610	529	15,993	215
1896	650	563	20,933	177
1897	693	563	23,065	182
1898	754	629	28,388	344
1899	763	640	29,428	823
1900	813	682	32,439	985
1901	891	709	37,908	1,068
1902	947	707	41,825	1,081
1903	1,003	734	51,319	1,265
1904	1,086	770	52,957	2,084
1905	1,158	783	54,145	2,403
1906	1,193	793	55,575	2,698
1907	1,240	838	60,836	2,391
1908	1,286	840	61,523	2,481
1909	1,267	811	60,701	2,333

[a]Source: Company reports in annual volumes of Poor, *Manual of Railroads.*

locomotives (95 percent) and freight cars (190 percent) far outrun the growth of mileage. Moreover, locomotives and freight cars individually are much larger by 1909 (and locomotives far more powerful) than in the late nineties so the increase in capacity is significantly greater than indicated by the change in numbers alone.

An outcome of capacity (and associated) changes is improvement in output per unit of resource, i.e., a rise in productivity. We will view productivity change here by the changes in output per mile of operated road. Table 3–4 provides the figures for passenger miles and freight ton miles per mile of operated road for the Illinois Central. Again a few earlier years are provided to set perspective, then the annual figures are given for 1896–1909. Passenger productivity doesn't change much before the 1890s. The extraordinary high level of 1894 (year ending 30 June 1894)

Table 3–4
Illinois Central
Passenger and Freight Output Per Mile of Road[a]

Year	Passenger Miles (000 per mile of road operated)	Freight Ton Miles
1869	55.21	262.46
1878	34.91	243.93
1888	54.82	392.83
1890	55.01	413.64
1894	110.00	505.68
1896	72.38	657.89
1897	68.04	721.48
1898	69.76	721.23
1899	73.17	762.76
1900	79.48	890.87
1901	88.71	952.83
1902	93.85	1,041.12
1903	106.09	1,205.82
1904	111.76	1,202.93
1905	133.40	1,270.98
1906	115.60	1,408.40
1907	130.40	1,508.21
1908	133.89	1,366.04
1909	130.13	1,328.84

[a]Underlying data is from annual volumes of Poor, *Manual of Railroads.*

is undoubtedly the result of the Chicago World's Fair. Between 1896 and 1909 passenger miles per mile of road increase by 80 percent. This compares with 56 percent for all U. S. roads (data from *Historical Statistics of the United States*) over the same period. Unlike passenger productivity, freight productivity (freight ton miles per mile) increases fairly significantly (58 percent) in the earlier period (1869–1890). The increase is much greater (129 percent to the 1907 peak) after 1896. This Illinois Central increase is double the increase for all U. S. roads (64 percent) for the same period.

An important result of Harriman's policies can be seen by examining the per-mile rates for passengers and freight on the Illinois Central during his tenure. Both actual and real (1890 = 100) rates for the Illinois Central for the years 1883–1909 are presented in Table 3–5. Harriman was often

Table 3–5
Illinois Central
Average Passenger and Freight Rates[a]

Year	Average Passenger Rates[b] per mile		Average Freight Rates[c] per ton mile	
	actual	1890 = 100[d]	actual	1890 = 100[d]
		(cents)		(cents)
1883	2.42	1.97	1.43	1.16
1884	2.28	2.01	1.37	1.21
1885	2.21	2.13	1.31	1.26
1886	2.21	2.21	1.16	1.16
1887	2.26	2.18	1.09	1.03
1888	1.75	1.67	0.95	0.91
1889	1.67	1.70	1.03	1.04
1890	2.08	2.08	0.95	0.95
1891	2.07	2.08	0.93	0.94
1892	2.10	2.26	0.91	0.98
1893	2.00	2.11	0.84	0.88
1894	1.92	2.25	0.83	0.97
1895	2.00	2.30	0.81	0.93
1896	1.98	2.39	0.74	0.80
1897	1.98	2.39	0.67	0.81
1898	1.94	2.25	0.70	0.81
1899	2.01	2.16	0.69	0.74
1900	2.02	2.02	0.65	0.65
1901	1.96	1.99	0.62	0.63
1902	2.00	1.91	0.62	0.59
1903	1.97	1.87	0.59	0.56
1904	1.97	1.85	0.61	0.57
1905	1.84	1.72	0.59	0.55
1906	1.96	1.78	0.56	0.51
1907	1.96	1.69	0.58	0.50
1908	1.86	1.66	0.59	0.53
1909	1.84	1.53	0.60	0.50

[a]Source: Annual volumes of Poor, *Manual of the Railroads.*
[b]Revenue per passenger mile.
[c]Revenue per freight ton mile.
[d]Warren and Pearson wholesale price index for 1883–1890 and Bureau of Labor Statistics. Wholesale price index for 1890–1909. Indexes linked at 1890 and 1890 set equal to 1.0.

accused of engaging in monopolistic practices; one might therefore expect rates for his railroads to remain relatively high and to decline (if at all) only very slowly. As Table 3–5 shows, the decline in both actual and real rates for the Illinois Central was substantial over the period. The 1909 average rate per passenger mile was 76 percent of the 1883 rate while the freight rate per ton mile was only 42 percent of 1883.

Table 3–6 shows the average passenger and freight rates for all U. S. railroads. Average passenger rates for all U. S. roads declined only slightly less than for the Illinois Central with 1909 being 80 percent of 1883. Freight rates on average for all U. S. roads declined much less than for the Illinois Central. The 1909 rate is 62 percent of 1883. The average freight rate per ton mile for all U. S. roads is 26 percent higher in 1909 than for the Illinois Central.

The freight rate comparison provides a clear indication of the benefit of Harriman's policies for the public. His efforts to make his roads the very best and to maintain them in that condition produced a relentless decline in both the actual and real cost of freight transportation. There is no clear differential between the movement of Illinois Central passenger rates and the average for all U. S. roads. The decline in passenger rates does not fully reflect the gain to the traveling public from Harriman's policies. Rail travel between 1883 and 1909 became significantly safer, more comfortable, and faster. These substantial, positive benefits to passengers are not reflected in the decline in rates. On the Illinois Central they were an outcome of Harriman's investment policies and concern with safety.

The Illinois Central performed much better in terms of both profitability and productivity change in the Harriman period than earlier. This is also reflected in the declining cost and rising quality of transportation services provided by the Illinois Central. One cannot attribute all of this change to the management of the Illinois Central and Harriman's contribution to that management, but given that the Illinois Central outperformed all U. S. roads on average by a significant margin it is clear that the Illinois Central management (and Harriman) was responsible for a major part of the improvement. Harriman was a major figure in Illinois Central management in this later period and increasingly so over time. Thus, his contributions at the Illinois Central are undoubtedly an important factor in its improved performance. His genius in railroad management and finance bore their first fruit at the Illinois Central with a subsequent abundant harvest from the great projects of Harriman's later career to which we will now turn.

Table 3–6
All U. S. Railroads
Average Passenger and Freight Rates[a]

Year	Passenger Revenue[b] per mile		Freight Revenue[c] per ton mile	
	actual	1890 = 100[d] (cents)	actual	1890 = 100[d] (cents)
1883	2.42	1.97	1.22	0.99
1884	2.36	2.08	1.12	0.99
1885	2.20	2.12	1.05	1.01
1886	2.19	2.19	1.04	1.04
1887	2.28	2.20	1.03	0.97
1888	2.24	2.16	0.98	0.94
1889	2.17	2.20	0.97	0.98
1890	2.17	2.17	0.94	1.00
1891	2.14	2.16	0.90	0.91
1892	2.13	2.29	0.90	0.97
1893	2.11	2.22	0.88	0.93
1894	1.99	2.34	0.86	1.01
1895	2.04	2.35	0.84	0.97
1896	2.02	2.44	0.81	0.98
1897	2.02	2.44	0.80	0.96
1898	1.97	2.28	0.75	0.87
1899	1.98	2.13	0.72	0.78
1900	2.00	2.00	0.73	0.73
1901	2.01	2.04	0.75	0.76
1902	1.99	1.90	0.76	0.73
1903	2.01	1.90	0.76	0.72
1904	2.01	1.89	0.78	0.73
1905	1.96	1.83	0.77	0.72
1906	2.00	1.82	0.75	0.68
1907	2.01	1.73	0.76	0.66
1908	1.94	1.73	0.75	0.67
1909	1.93	1.60	0.76	0.63

[s]Source: *Historical Statistics of the United States: Colonial Times to 1970,* U. S. Department of Commerce, Bureau of the Census (Washington, D. C.: Government Printing Office, 1975).

[b]Revenue per passenger mile.

[c]Revenue per freight ton mile.

[d]Warren and Pearson, Wholesale price index for 1883–1890 and Bureau of Labor Statistics Wholesale Price Index 1890–1909. Indexes linked at 1890 and 1890 set equal to 1.0. Indexes from *Historical Statistics of the United States.*

CHAPTER FOUR

Applying the Lessons: The Union Pacific, 1897–1909

Reorganization

The Union Pacific operated on the verge of insolvency from its inception until its financial collapse in 1893. The relatively high cost of initial construction and the substantial debt incurred both on the private first mortgage and the second mortgage held by the U. S. government created a situation where holding off financial insolvency became one of management's primary tasks. The cost of the Union Pacific in 1870 was reported to be $106.2 million or $102,951 per mile. The various mortgages totaled $71,845 per mile. Net earnings in 1873 and 1874 were $4.1 million and $5.3 million respectively, while interest on the funded debt excluding the government debt (second mortgage) was $3.4 million per year. During the 1870s earnings increased substantially and the margin of earnings over what had to be immediately paid out in debt interest grew.

The passage of the Thurman Act in 1879 posed an additional financial burden on the affected railroads including the Union Pacific. Under the Pacific Railroad Acts of 1862 and 1864 the Union Pacific was required to set aside 5 percent of net earnings, plus one-half the sums due it from the U. S. for government transportation, for retirement of the bond loan provided by the Acts. The Thurman bill provided that the other half of the sums due for government transportation would go into a sinking fund for retirement of the debt to the government. In addition, if the 5 percent of net earnings and the sums due for government transportation did not

49

total 25 percent of net earnings, an additional payment (not to exceed $850,000 for the Union Pacific) would be required to bring the companies' payment up to 25 percent of net earnings. The funds paid under the 1862 and 1864 Acts, in effect, went into a sinking fund that paid no interest. This was a significant financial handicap to the railroads involved. Under the Thurman Act the additional payments went into a sinking fund based on government bonds. This returned interest, but only 2.5 to 3 percent compared to the 6 percent interest on the subsidy bonds themselves. This burden was reduced by an act of Congress in 1887 which allowed the sinking fund to purchase first-mortgage bonds of the railroads themselves.

The Thurman Act still operated as a financial handicap to the Union Pacific after the 1887 change. This is because the funds going into the sinking fund under the Thurman Act could have been invested in the railroad itself at a much higher rate of return than that obtained from the sinking fund. The requirements of both the 1862 and 1864 Acts and the Thurman Act undercut the financial well-being of the Union Pacific.

In 1880 the Union Pacific was consolidated with the Kansas Pacific and Denver Pacific railroads. The Kansas Pacific had been in a chronic state of insolvency. With the help of a little coercion, Jay Gould demonstrated in the late 1870s the wisdom of the Union Pacific's purchase of his lines at his absurd terms. This aggregation of some strength with considerable weakness profited at the time only the holders of Kansas Pacific and Denver Pacific stock, i.e., primarily Jay Gould. Gould was the chief holder of the Kansas Pacific and held virtually all the Denver Pacific stock. The effect of the consolidation was to increase significantly the value of Gould's holdings. The result of this substantial merger and the resultant expansion of its lines was that the new Union Pacific Railway Company in 1880 was in worse shape than its predecessor, the Union Pacific Railroad Company. The bonded indebtedness of the new road was approximately equal per mile (but now there were 779 more miles) to that of the old: $70,453 compared to $71,845. The added mileage had on average less capacity to pay its bonded indebtness than the old Union Pacific.

In the eighties the Union Pacific constructed or acquired a number of branch lines. The most important new construction was the Oregon Short Line, organized in 1881 to tap the business of Washington and Oregon. The 1880 consolidation with its load of added debt and worthless branches, intensifying competition among the transcontinental railroads, and the economic slowdown in the economy as a whole in the early eighties all combined to diminish the margin of earnings over debt payments toward zero. The severity of the situation is even clearer when one recalls that the Union Pacific was not even paying the annual interest on about one-third of its debt (the U. S. government debt—second mortgage).

In 1884 Sidney Dillon resigned as president of the Union Pacific and Charles Francis Adams, Jr. was elected his successor. Adams instituted major economies in the operation of the road and was able to reduce significantly the floating debt. Fixed charges did not decrease enough to help, declining only from $7.6 million per year when Adams became president, to $7.3 million five years later. Net earnings declined from $11.4 million in 1884 to $10.3 million in 1889 and $9.6 million in 1890. Part of the problem was the rapid decline in rates everywhere during the eighties and nineties. Funded debt in the Adams period was reduced from $90.8 million in 1884 to $82.1 million in 1889 and $74 million in 1890 as the company steadily bought up its own debt. The major effort that Adams undertook to save the company was a rapid extension of its branch mileage. Between 1884 and 1890 a total of 3,132 miles were built or acquired, all under separate organizations. Floating debt of the Union Pacific reached $21.4 million in 1891. A substantial portion of this ($15 million according to the government directors) was the result of the branch-line extension. In 1889 the Union Pacific added the important connecting line of the Oregon Railway & Navigation Company which secured it a firm foothold in the traffic of the Pacific Northwest and made it a significant competitor for that business with the Great Northern and the Northern Pacific. Because of the method of payment for the Oregon Railway & Navigation stock held by Henry Villard of the Northern Pacific, the Union Pacific's floating debt was substantially increased.

By 1892 the Union Pacific was in dire financial straits. Its earnings had been nearly constant for five years and uncomfortably little above fixed charges so that a large floating debt had been created. Three-year collateral notes had been issued in 1891 under a scheme of Gould's to postpone the payment of the floating debt. These were to mature in 1894. The principal ($33.5 million) on the second mortgage (the government debt) was to mature between 1 November 1895 and 1 January 1899. After deduction of sums already paid to the government and addition of interest paid annually by the government during the debt's life, the grand total owed was approximately $52 million.

The year 1893 saw a severe downturn in the national economy and its resultant impact on the transportation business and railroad earnings. During the year both gross and net earnings of the Union Pacific declined precipitately. As the year wore on, the magnitude of the projected deficit of fixed payments over earnings expanded to $3 million or more.

A receivership was the only means available to prevent the breakup of the system and to protect the interests of all the creditors. Thus, in October 1893 the Union Pacific entered into receivership, closing a long struggle to maintain the road's solvency. From the first, the primary goals of the projected reorganization were holding the system and its earning capacity together while simultaneously bringing about a permanent reduction in fixed charges. In addition, the government debt and the floating debt had to be paid off.

Starting in 1893 and continuing through 1897, two different comprehensive reorganization committees and several special interest committees worked at the creation of a plan acceptable to a majority of the creditors. While these negotiations and efforts in Congress to pass a bill providing for the refunding of the government debt proceeded with agonizing slowness, the system itself began to disintegrate. Loss of branch lines occurred both because the receivers wished to get rid of branches and contracts that were burdensome and because bondholders of subsidiary roads refused to wait for congressional action and insisted on foreclosure of the liens. The Union Pacific receivers cast out the Leavenworth, Topeka & Southwestern in March 1894. Separate receivers were appointed for the Union Pacific, Denver & Gulf; the Fort Worth & Denver City Railway Company; the Denver, Leadville & Gunnison; and the St. Joseph & Grand Island in October 1893. Separate receivers were also appointed for the Oregon Railway & Navigation Company in June 1894. The net result of the actions was a reduction in the mileage of the Union Pacific from 8,167 in late 1893 to 4,469 in May 1895. At the latter time proceedings against the Oregon Short Line endangered an additional 1,424 miles.

Given these difficulties and the refusal of Congress to pass a government debt refunding bill, the general reorganization committee was disbanded in March 1895. A new general reorganization committee was formed in late 1895 and included among others Jacob H. Schiff of Kuhn, Loeb & Company as the financial manager in place of J. P. Morgan. Schiff was to play an important role in later Union Pacific affairs and various activities of Harriman. The new committee's eventual plan contained three noteworthy points: (1) a foreclosure sale was expected; (2) no definite provision was made for government debt: and (3) it did not attempt to meet the collateral trust notes of 1891. The detailed plan for reorganization was a strong one, reducing fixed charges from $7 million to an eventual lower limit of $3 million. By January 1896 the committee had obtained a majority of the shares and first mortgage and the agreement of others to its plan.

The plan did not meet with the approval of the second mortgage (the U. S. government). A renewed proposition for refunding the government debt was defeated in the House in 1896, and in January 1897 the government agreed to join with the receivers if they would guarantee a cash bid at least equal to the original amount of government bonds less payments already made. Despairing of any better terms, the reorganization committee accepted this first affirmative action by the government. The cash requirement after sinking fund assets, etc. was $28.7 million.

In August 1897 foreclosure of the Union Pacific main line was ordered in all states through which it passed. Because the government found the foreclosure decrees unsatisfactory to some extent, it prepared to appeal the foreclosure. The reorganization committee then increased its bid by $4 million. The government was still not prepared to allow the sale and gave notice of application for postponement to 15 December. The reorganization committee then raised its additional bid by $8 million. The property was finally sold under foreclosure on 1 and 2 November 1897. The price paid was a little over $81.5 million.

During its first year the work of the second reorganization committee had proceeded smoothly. However, in the latter part of 1896 it had become clear to Schiff and his associates that some powerful influence was opposing them in both the Pacific Roads Commission and Congress. The initial thought was that J. P. Morgan desired to regain control of the reorganization. Schiff ascertained from Morgan himself that this was not the case. Morgan promised to investigate to determine the source of opposition. In a short time he was able to inform Schiff that the source of his difficulty was E. H. Harriman.

Confronting Harriman with this allegation, Schiff was informed by Harriman that he (Harriman) was indeed the opposition and that the reason for his opposition was his wish to reorganize the Union Pacific himself. There is reason to believe that Harriman's original intention was to unite the Illinois Central and the Union Pacific. Because the presidents of the New York Central and the Chicago & Northwestern were prominent members of the reorganization committee, Harriman may have feared that controlling influence in the Union Pacific would go to those roads, thus shutting out the Illinois Central. After he became a director of the Union Pacific Harriman seems to have abandoned any idea of a consolidation between it and the Illinois Central.

Because Schiff refused to make Harriman chairman of the executive committee of the reorganized Union Pacific, the first discussion between the two did not resolve Harriman's opposition. Since this opposition continued and intensified, Schiff in a second discussion proposed a compromise that Harriman accepted. The compromise was that Harriman would be made a director of the reorganized company and a member of the executive committee. In that way if he proved to be the strongest committee member he would probably get the chairmanship he desired. Harriman initially put up $900,000 upon joining the financing syndicate for the reorganization.

The risk involved in purchasing the main line of the Union Pacific was substantial. The road was in poor physical condition and lacked adequate equipment. Its through line to the Pacific Northwest as well as all its Nebraska and Kansas branches had been lost.

Reassembling the Pieces and Reconstruction

On 6 December 1897 when the new Union Pacific Company completed its organization, Harriman was elected a director and soon thereafter a member of the executive committee. As a newcomer, Harriman was initially viewed somewhat askance by his new colleagues. Apparently he did not spend any time brooding about this, but in his early months on the board plunged into an intensive study of the Union Pacific and its needs. In May 1898 Harriman was elected chairman of the executive committee of the Union Pacific. Also in this early period he bought all the Union Pacific common stock that he could at prices up to 25 and it was this stock that provided the basis for his eventual great wealth. John Moody calculated that someone who purchased 100 shares of Union Pacific stock in 1898 for $1,600 would have received over the next eight and a half years dividends and capital gain of $21,900 and was then receiving 63 percent on the original investment.

The reorganized Union Pacific began operation on 1 January 1898.

The new road lacked the great subsidiaries of its predecessor: the Oregon Short Line, the Oregon Railway & Navigation Company, and the Union Pacific, Denver & Gulf, all of which had been reorganized separately taking a total of 4,307 miles out of the Union Pacific system. Most branch lines reorganized independently or were still in the hands of receivers. Altogether the Union Pacific had lost 5,832 miles of its former system. The reorganized road had 1,849 miles of railway. The first major task confronting the new company was reacquisition of its important branches and feeders. It took almost three years to bring most of these back into the fold and one subsidiary, the St. Joseph & Grand Island, was not added until 1906.

In December 1897 the reorganization committee had obtained $8.5 million of $24.8 million of the capital stock of the reorganized Oregon Short Line Railroad Company. In January 1899 the shareholders of the Union Pacific ratified a proposal to increase Union Pacific common stock by $27.5 million and to offer the new shares in exchange for that amount of Oregon Short Line stock. This offer was accepted by Oregon Short Line shareholders who also paid $3 for each share exchanged. On the New York Stock Exchange the average closing bid for Union Pacific common in January 1899 was $45.68. Using this to value the exchange, the net cost of the Oregon Short Line acquisition to the Union Pacific was $11.5 million or $7,567 per mile.

Union Pacific shareholders in October 1899 authorized additional preferred stock of $25 million and common stock of $7.7 million. The former was offered in exchange for the Oregon Railway & Navigation Company's preferred stock ($11 million par) and the outstanding "Income B" bonds of the Oregon Short Line held by the former road. The common stock ($16.3 million par) of the Navigation Company had been the collateral for the "Income B" bonds so this offer which was accepted gave the Union Pacific a firm hold on that common stock. The $7.7 million of new Union Pacific common was offered in exchange for an equal quantity (the remainder) of the Navigation Company's common stock. The average closing bid for Union Pacific preferred in New York was 76.375 and for common 44.50 during October 1899. These values are used to value the stock exchange to obtain the Navigation Company. The Union Pacific also purchased the Northern Pacific's holding of the Navigation Company's preferred stock for $1.8 million, making the total cost of acquisition of the Oregon Railway & Navigation Company $24.3 million or $22,788 per mile.

Also during 1898 a large number of former Union Pacific branches were purchased at foreclosure. The apparent cost of these purchases aggregating 1,401 miles of railway is $9.6 million or $6,852 per mile.

While acquisition of former branches was underway, Harriman was planning the reconstruction and reequipment of the Union Pacific. In the summer of 1898 Harriman with his two older daughters, President Burt, Chief Engineer Berry, and a few other high officials of the Union Pacific made a daylight examination of the entire Union Pacific line from the Missouri River to the Pacific. This was done on a special train comprised of an observation car in front and a locomotive in the rear. The purpose was a visual examination of grades, curves, rails, ballast, etc. The journey, accomplished only in daylight and punctuated with stops at important stations to question officials, took several weeks.

Harriman's personal inspection trip thoroughly convinced him of the poor state of the Union Pacific's road and equipment. The major tasks that he determined needed to be accomplished were: (1) replacement of small and light freight cars; (2) reduction of grades; (3) improvement of curves; (4) replacement of existing locomotives with larger, heavier models, and (5) replacement of light rail with heavy rail and along with this improvement of the ballast.

While in Portland, Harriman telegraphed the board in New York for authority to spend up to $25 million for improvements and equipment for the Union Pacific. Upon his return to New York in late summer he submitted his detailed argument for the expenditure to the board and gained their approval after long and strenuous discussion.

The improvements that Harriman sought, and in particular the larger and more powerful locomotives coupled with significant grade reduction and curve improvement, promised substantial increases in productivity (reductions in cost) for the Union Pacific. Harriman was a major exponent of this approach to productivity improvement (cost reduction). The impression he made on his board colleagues was apparently profound. Not only did they approve his reconstruction proposal, but on 1 December 1898 he was elected chairman of the board as well as chairman of the executive committee. After only a year on the board he had attained supreme control of Union Pacific affairs.

The reconstruction effort began 1 March 1899. In addition to larger, heavier cars and more powerful locomotives, a major goal was grade reduction. Harriman wanted a maximum grade of 43 feet to the mile and this was adopted as the standard for the road. Achieving this was not easy, especially in the mountains west of Cheyenne. The greatest achievement was reducing the maximum grade on the 18-mile stretch into Laramie from 98 feet per mile to 43 feet per mile. Only on two short stretches of road were maximum grades of more than 43 feet retained. Between Omaha and Ogden the Union Pacific reconstruction abandoned 150 miles of the old line and by rebuilding it in new locations saved twenty-two complete circles of curvature and nearly forty miles in distance.

The impact of Harriman's reconstruction of the Union Pacific can be seen from some simple comparisons. Between 1898 and 1909 the average weight of Union Pacific locomotives increased from 37 to 68 tons while the total capacity of the company's freight cars grew from 414,858 tons to 984,923 tons. The number of freight ton miles increased 64 percent between 1899 and 1909 while mileage increased only 12 percent. In 1899 the average freight car carried 12 tons and the average train had 29 cars while by 1907 the average car held 21 tons and the average train had 32 cars. The average number of passengers per train doubled, from 33 to 66 between 1899 and 1907.

Changes in equipment were an important part of the reconstruction program. Table 4–1 shows Union Pacific equipment figures for the years 1898 to 1909. There is a sharp rise in all categories of rolling stock over the period with the sharpest rise in 1907–1909. These of course are simply numbers and don't tell us the full story of the change in capacity. For instance, we noted above that the capacity of the company's freight cars more than doubled while in terms of actual numbers freight cars increased only 12 percent. Prior to 1907 there are some year-to-year declines in the number of specific types of equipment, but these do not indicate a fall in capacity. The numbers of Table 4–1 are incomplete by themselves, but do show a significant equipment increase for the Union Pacific during Harriman's management.

Rebuilding and reequipping the railroad were impressive feats. Less outwardly impressive but equally necessary were adequate ongoing maintenance and repair. Harriman saw to it that expenditures for these purposes were adequate to keep the road in first-class condition once he got it there. One reason he found the road in such poor physical condition was the very inadequate maintenance during the receivership. Between 1 January 1893 and 3 June 1898 only about $1 million was spent on maintenance and repair, a mere $179 yearly per mile for maintenance, betterments, and renewal of equipment.

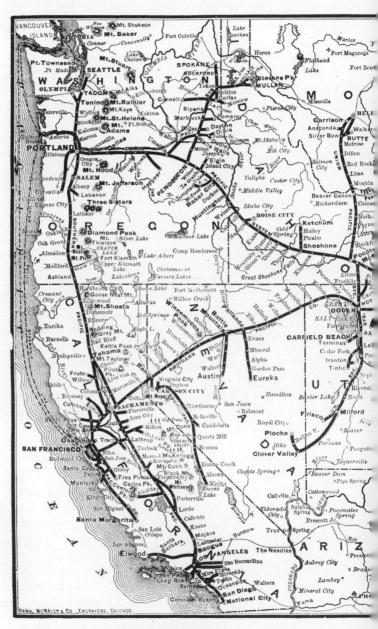

2. The Union Pacific Railroad

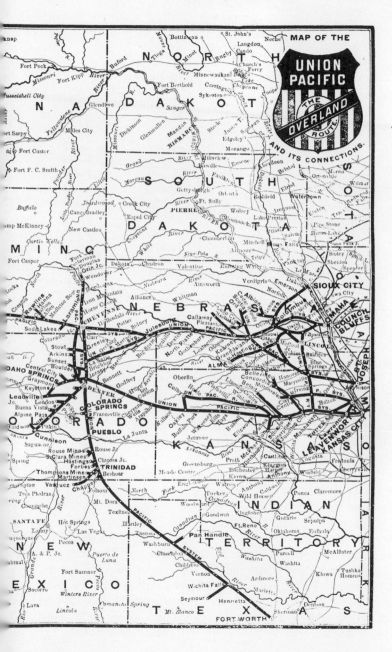

Table 4–1
Union Pacific System
Rolling Stock[a]

Year	Locomotives	Passenger cars	Freight cars	Service cars
1899	785	428	23,688	989
1900	775	573	22,243	1,640
1901	841	568	22,266	2,159
1902	787	580	21,081	2,702
1903	824	566	21,071	2,431
1904	856	557	22,038	2,439
1905	835	566	22,406	2,434
1906	881	580	23,637	2,454
1907	1,051	643	25,377	2,929
1908	1,088	703	25,488	3,598
1909	1,088	711	26,470	3,728

[a]From annual reports in Poor, *Manual of Railroads*.

Reaping the Harvest

The result of the reconstruction of the Union Pacific and ongoing economic growth in its service area was a veritable torrent of earnings. For the fiscal year 1899 (ending 30 June) the current dollar value of capital earnings was $15.2 million. In 1909 current dollar capital earnings totaled $37.3 million, an increase of 145 percent. This is more than double the rate of increase for all U. S. roads shown by the estimates of *Historical Statistics of the United States*. Table 4–2 presents Union Pacific real dollar (1900 = 100) investment cost and capital earnings for 1886 to 1896 and 1 January 1898 to (30 June) 1909. Real capital earnings rose from $16.3 million in 1899 to $30.9 million in 1909, an increase of 90 percent. Thus, even with the effect of the price level rise taken out, we see a very substantial rise in capital earnings. The internal rate of return on operations (excluding investment income) for the Union Pacific is 7.5 percent for 1886–1896 and 10.6 percent for 1898–1909. The economic rate of return on Union Pacific operations was increased 44 percent in the Harriman era despite the substantial investment ($119.2 million current dollars for betterments and equipment in addition to purchase of roads) during that period. This is a significant change and achievement. To a considerable extent this was the product of Harriman's management.

Table 4–2
Union Pacific System
Capital Earnings and Investment Cost[a]
(000 of 1900$)

Year	Investment Costs	Capital Earnings
1886	122,020[b]	8,850
1887	6,936	10,481
1888	3,821	9,953
1889	156	13,784
1890	895	12,214
1891	0	13,607
1892	888	15,452
1893	0	10,778
1894	0	7,656
1895	0	10,473
1896	977	10,860
1897	—	—
1898	105,459[d]	5,238[c]
1899		
1900	8,977	17,720
1901	12,260	19,220
1902	5,540	20,896
1903	5,302	20,789
1904	6,363	22,462
1905	4,507	25,656
1906	6,405	27,543
1907	24,743	28,766
1908	11,410	28,368
1909	10,687	30,943

[a]Figures for 1886–1889 from Lloyd J. Mercer, *Railroads and Land Grant Policy: A Study in Government Intervention* (New York: Academic Press, 1982), 164, 182. Data for 1890–1909 derived from company reports in annual volumes of Poor, *Manual of Railroads.*

[b]Includes 1886 capital stock from Lloyd J. Mercer, op. cit.

[c]For six months to 30 June 1898.

[d]Capital value.

Another view of the rate of return is provided by Table 4–3 where the gross accounting rate of return is presented for the two time periods. The gross accounting rate of return for 1886–1896 is 8.5 percent compared with 11.34 percent for 1898–1909. The latter is one-third higher than the former, supporting the view and conclusion derived from the internal rate of return calculation above.

The reconstruction of the Union Pacific (and the associated rebuilding of the Central Pacific Railroad and other components of the Southern Pa-

Table 4–3
Union Pacific System
Gross Accounting Rate of Return

Year	Gross Capital (1900 $)	Capital Earnings (1900 $)	Gross Accounting Rate of Return
1886	122,020	8,856	7.26
1887	128,956	10,481	8.13
1888	132,777	9,953	7.50
1889	132,933	13,784	10.37
1890	133,828	12,214	9.13
1891	133,828	13,607	10.17
1892	134,716	14,452	11.47
1893	134,716	10,772	8.00
1894	134,716	7,656	5.68
1895	134,716	10,473	7.77
1896	135,693	10,860	8.00
Mean rate of return			8.50
1898	105,459	5,238	9.93[a]
1899	160,403	16,340	10.19
1900	169,380	17,720	10.46
1901	181,640	19,220	10.58
1902	187,180	20,896	11.16
1903	192,482	20,789	10.80
1904	198,845	22,462	11.30
1905	203,352	25,656	12.62
1906	209,757	27,543	13.13
1907	234,500	28,766	12.27
1908	245,910	28,368	11.54
1909	256,597	30,943	12.06
Mean rate of return			11.34

[a]annual rate

cific System) raised productivity as well as profits, thus benefiting rail-road users (society) as well as investors. Table 4–4 gives a picture of the productivity impact of the reconstruction and other management endeavors of Harriman with the Union Pacific. If we take the peak figure (1893) of the earlier period (1886–1896), passenger miles per mile of road in that period rose 18 percent. Between the end points, freight ton miles per mile of road rose 40 percent during the period. In the Harriman period output per mile of road rose 150 percent for passengers and 71 percent (to the 1907 peak) for freight. Some substantial part of these enormous productivity increases was the result of Harriman's management.

Table 4–4
Union Pacific System
Passenger and Freight Output Per Mile of Road[a]
(000 per mile of road)

	Passenger Miles		Freight Ton Miles	
Year	Union Pacific System	All U.S. Roads	Union Pacific System	All U.S. Roads
1886	54.86	57.52	279.73	314.40
1887	56.87	57.16	322.32	332.88
1888	56.90	58.48	333.83	341.86
1889	48.15	59.16	278.37	339.84
1890	52.84	59.28	308.10	381.27
1891	44.66	61.69	314.91	390.82
1892	45.86	66.80	325.00	418.10
1893	64.84	64.13	366.08	349.59
1894	47.16	62.18	355.52	365.35
1895	44.77	52.25	395.06	398.63
1896	45.09	54.57	391.81	393.12
1899	52.47	58.33	592.51	494.38
1900	60.79	61.97	662.06	547.16
1901	59.91	65.40	671.24	554.27
1902	70.12	72.80	751.10	573.64
1903	82.85	73.68	698.60	610.19
1904	91.00	73.80	757.20	587.47
1905	98.79	77.58	899.82	607.77
1906	118.90	79.37	990.63	680.82
1907	120.15	84.52	1010.46	721.40
1908	131.56	87.17	912.46	654.53
1909	131.18	85.03	867.81	639.12

[a]Underlying data for Union Pacific System from annual volumes of Poor, *Manual of Railroads* and for all U.S. roads from *Historical Statistics of the United States*.

It will help to put these numbers in perspective to compare them with the average change for all U. S. roads. Table 4–4 also provides passenger miles per mile of road and freight ton miles per mile of road for all U. S. roads. Freight output per mile of road for all U. S. roads increased 46 percent between 1899 and the 1907 peak, while passenger output also rose 46 percent from 1899 to 1909. Average freight output per mile rose 54 percent more on the Union Pacific than on all U. S. roads while average passenger output per mile rose 226 percent more. Freight output per mile was 20 percent more than the U. S. average in 1899 and 36 percent more in 1909. The comparable figures for passengers are 10 percent *less* in 1899 and 54 percent *more* in 1909. Harriman's reconstruction of the Union Pacific paid handsome dividends to society as well as to Union Pacific investors.

The reorganized Union Pacific paid its first dividend (1 1/2 percent on preferred stock) in fiscal 1898 (year ending 30 June). The preferred dividend rose to 3.5 percent in 1900, rose to 4.0 percent in 1901, then continued at that level for the remainder of the period. A common stock dividend of 3.5 percent was paid in fiscal 1900. In 1901 this was raised to 4 percent and continued through 1904. The common dividend was increased to 4.5 percent in fiscal 1905, 6.0 in 1906, 7 percent in 1907, and 10 percent in fiscal 1908. Since the 10 percent dividend was made in August 1906, the calendar year dividend became 10 percent in 1907.

The movement of average rates per passenger mile and per ton mile provides another view of the impact of Harriman's policies with the Union Pacific. Table 4–5 presents the actual and real rates for the Union Pacific over the period 1899–1909. The 1909 passenger rate is 73 percent of 1899. This represents a very substantial and swift decline. Over the same period the average freight rate per ton mile declined significantly with the 1909 level also falling to 73 percent of 1899.

Despite the rapid decline, both the average passenger and freight ton miles rates of the Union Pacific in 1909 are above the average for all U. S. roads (see Table 3–6). This was quite typical for western roads where traffic density was lighter than in the East or for all U. S roads on average. The Union Pacific passenger rate is 15 percent higher while the rate per freight ton mile is 35 percent higher than the average for all U. S. roads. The fall in the rates over 1899–1909 is about the same for the passenger rate for the Union Pacific and all U. S. roads, and faster for the rate per freight ton mile for the Union Pacific than all U. S. roads. Undoubtedly, a major factor in the Union Pacific rates being higher than the U. S. average has to do with the density of traffic. Traffic was spread

Table 4–5
Union Pacific
Average Passenger and Freight Rates[a]

Year	Average Passenger Rates[b] per mile		Average Freight Rates[c] per ton mile	
	actual	1900 = 100[d]	actual	1900 = 100[d]
		(cents)		(cents)
1899	2.33	2.51	1.09	1.17
1900	2.23	2.23	0.96	0.96
1901	2.24	2.27	1.00	1.01
1902	2.25	2.14	0.98	0.93
1903	2.16	2.03	0.96	0.90
1904	2.15	2.02	0.97	0.91
1905	2.14	2.00	0.89	0.83
1906	2.06	1.87	0.91	0.83
1907	2.19	1.88	0.96	0.83
1908	2.19	1.95	1.00	0.89
1909	2.22	1.84	1.03	0.85

[a]Source: Annual volumes of Poor, *Manual of Railroads.*
[b]*Revenue per passenger mile.*
[c]*Revenue per freight ton mile.*
[d]*Based on Bureau of Labor Statistics Wholesale price index from Historical Statistics of the United States* with 1900 set equal to 100.

very much more thinly for the Union Pacific than for all U. S. roads on average. The difference in the character of traffic is also a factor. For the Union Pacific, the proportion of cheap rate (bulk) goods, e.g., coal, was much less than for the U. S. average. This would surely have added to average costs and average rates.

In evaluating Harriman's performance with the Union Pacific, one might argue that it is easier for a reorganizer of a badly run-down railroad to show dramatic changes than for the manager of an established road. Some comparisons with other transcontinentals will be helpful here. The following internal rates of return have been estimated for major transcontinentals to 1900: the Great Northern, 8.7 percent; Northern Pacific, 6.3 percent; Atchison, Topeka and Santa Fe, 6.1 percent; and Canadian Pacific, 3.9 percent.[1] The Union Pacific rate of return under Harriman is 22 percent higher than the highest of these, the Great Northern, and about 70 percent higher than the next two. This suggests that the Union Pacific's performance is the result of something more than what was common to western transcontinentals of the period. What the Union Pacific had that these other roads did not enjoy was the benefit of Harriman's management and financial genius.

Harriman's management created a revitalized and much more productive Union Pacific. A railroad that had barely kept its head above water in the preceding quarter century became a high-paying investment with a solid cushion of earning power between it and insolvency. The legacy of Harriman's management was a Union Pacific serving its territory with greatly increased productivity and paying investors a handsome return on their money.

CHAPTER FIVE

Combining Systems: The Southern Pacific, 1901–1909

The fundamental progenitor of the Southern Pacific of 1901 was the Central Pacific Railroad organized 28 June 1861 by the engineer Theodore Judah. The Central Pacific was to be the western portion of the first transcontinental railroad soon to be subsidized by the Pacific Railroad Acts of 1862 and 1864. In 1860 Judah had discovered a practical route for a railroad over the Sierra Nevada. With this key bit of information to clinch his proposition, Judah attempted to interest capitalists in San Francisco and Sacramento in financing his project. He was unsuccessful in San Francisco, but struck a responsive chord in Sacramento where enough interest was generated that a group of people including the "Big Four"—Leland Stanford, Charles Crocker, Collis P. Huntington, and Mark Hopkins—formed the company and raised the money for a full instrumental survey from Sacramento to the Truckee River in the summer of 1861. The line then surveyed is still today the general line of the Central Pacific.

After the 1861 survey the Sacramento capitalists now led by Huntington and his friends were inclined to see the project through if sufficient government assistance could be secured. Judah then journeyed to Washington to lobby for the necessary legislation which was forthcoming in the Pacific Railroad Acts of 1862 and 1864.

Construction of the Central Pacific began 8 January 1863 at Sacramento. By January 1868 the Central Pacific was opened to the California state line, 278 miles from Sacramento. The race with the Union Pacific for bond and land subsidy, which were tied to mileage constructed, was then on in earnest with 362 miles of road built in 1868. The summit of Promontory Point was attained 30 April 1869 and the famous golden spike ceremony on 10 May signaled completion of the first transcontinental railroad with the linkup of the Central and the Union Pacific Railroads. The Central Pacific added 47.5 miles from Promontory Point to 5 miles west of Ogden by purchasing the line from the Union Pacific. Later the Central Pacific leased the remaining five miles into Ogden for 999 years, establishing the final junction of the Central and the Union Pacific.

Even before the completion of the transcontinental line, the Big Four were spreading their railroad system with the acquisition of four railroads before 1867: the Western Pacific, the California & Oregon, the California Central, and the Yuba. In 1868 the San Francisco & San Jose and Southern Pacific Railroad were added to the Big Four's collection. These two roads plus the Santa Clara & Pajaro Valley Railroad and the California Southern were consolidated in 1870 into the Southern Pacific of California. Over the next few years construction of the Southern Pacific proceeded down the San Joaquin Valley to Los Angeles, then through the Imperial Valley, reaching Fort Yuma in 1877. The Southern Pacific of Arizona and the Southern Pacific of New Mexico were built next starting in 1878 with the latter reaching El Paso, Texas, on 19 May 1881.

Huntington, the leader of the Central Pacific–Southern Pacific interests, took control of the Galveston, Harrisburg & San Antonio Railroad and used the resulting financial leverage to produce an agreement between the road and Jay Gould of the Texas & Pacific by which the Texas & Pacific gave up its corporate rights west of El Paso and the two roads were operated as a continuous line. Huntington next purchased Morgan's Louisiana and Texas lines which enabled the Southern Pacific to enter New Orleans. By January 1883 through cars ran between San Francisco and New Orleans on what became the Sunset Route of the Southern Pacific. This then offered an alternate transcontinental route to the Central Pacific–Union Pacific route.

The various parts of the system described were held together by a combination of leases and stock control. By 1877 the Huntington group held all or a majority of the stock in all companies in the system. Initially the Central Pacific was the lessee. The only exception was the Northern Division of the Southern Pacific of California which was never leased to the Central Pacific. In 1884 a new firm, the Southern Pacific Company was incorporated in Kentucky as a holding company for the associates' empire. The Southern Pacific Company leased the Southern Pacific of

California and the subsidiaries comprising the through lines to New Orleans for 99 years from 10 February 1885. The Central Pacific was also leased for 99 years from 1 April 1885. Prior to this, the Southern Pacific Company issued $100 million in capital stock and acquired in exchange for its certificates the capital stock of the three Southern Pacific Railroads (California, Arizona, and New Mexico).

The apparent reason for creation of the holding company (the Southern Pacific Company) was that by 1884 the ownership of Central Pacific stock had become scattered, Huntington and his associates retaining less than 30 percent of the stock. The reason for this was the creation of an active market for Central Pacific shares before one developed for Southern Pacific shares. In the late seventies and early eighties sale of Central Pacific stock by the associates was a major means of financing the expansion of their system. Thus, the railroad system controlled by the Southern Pacific Company was truly a product of the Central Pacific Railroad.

By 1899 the Central Pacific Railroad had become an obstacle to Harriman. Reconstruction of the Union Pacific was an impressive engineering and management feat. The finished product suffered from one substantial flaw. That shortcoming was the Central Pacific Railroad built over thirty years earlier between Sacramento and Ogden. The Central Pacific was burdened with steep grades and excessive curvature. While Harriman had doubled the capacity of the Union Pacific between Ogden and Omaha, the Central Pacific as a major transcontinental feeder for the Union Pacific still had the capacity essentially put in place in 1863–1869. If the Central Pacific remained unimproved, the augmented capacity of the Union Pacific would be underutilized and its ability to pay for itself would be seriously crimped. The Central Pacific with its excess of short curves, grades up to 90 feet to the mile, and light rolling stock of limited capacity, could handle but a fraction of the transcontinental traffic of which the Union Pacific was capable.

Harriman had no control over the Central Pacific. Those who did exercise such control had plans for reconstruction, but found themselves short of the financial wherewithal to accomplish those plans. The reason for this state of affairs was that in the late nineties the Central Pacific owners, like the Union Pacific, had to resolve the government debt (second mortgage) of approximately $59 million on their property which was falling due between 1893 and 1899. After gaining control of the Union Pacific, Harriman made several efforts to buy the Central Pacific. The Southern Pacific Company would not sell. With the Central Pacific and the Sunset Route the Southern Pacific Company exercised considerable control over the central and southern transcontinental routes. It was clearly not in the Southern Pacific's interest to give up one of these two legs. To do so would tremendously increase the competitive pressure on the other and reduce the strong competitive position held by the Southern Pacific.

The opportunity to have complete control of his own destiny was presented to Harriman following the death of Collis P. Huntington on 13 August 1900. Huntington had been the leader and the strength of the Big Four who had built the Central Pacific. The leverage (and financial muscle) thereby gained had given them control of the Southern Pacific and the holding company, the Southern Pacific Company. He was also the last survivor, the others having died between 1878 and 1893. Huntington himself held 400,000 shares of Southern Pacific Company stock. He left two-thirds of the stock to his widow and one-third to a nephew. Both proved willing, even eager, to dispose of their holdings.

In February 1901 negotiations with the Huntingtons and with Edwin Hawley, Collis Huntington's closest business associate, proved fruitful and the Union Pacific was able to obtain 475,000 shares of Southern Pacific stock. This with shares obtained from others by Kuhn, Loeb & Company gave a total of 677,700 shares to the Union Pacific. Market quotations were around 45 for Southern Pacific stock, but the average cost of the shares thus acquired was 40.61. Kuhn, Loeb & Company agreed to deliver an additional 72,300 shares at the same price by 4 March 1901. This brought Union Pacific holdings to 750,000 shares which represented 38 percent of the outstanding capital stock of the Southern Pacific Company. While this did not provide absolute control, it was enough to prevent any other interest from gaining such control. The Union Pacific soon obtained another 150,000 shares of common stock and 180,000 shares of preferred, giving it 1,080,000 out of 2,374,000 shares, or 45.49 percent of the total. For all intents and purposes the Union Pacific and the Southern Pacific were then united under the same management.

The funds for purchase of control of the Southern Pacific Company were provided by the Union Pacific's issuance in 1901 of a new $100 million convertible bonds issue. The bonds were convertible (at par) any time within five years into common stock of the Union Pacific. Funds from these bonds also were used to purchase the Northern Pacific stock which became the basis for the Northern Securities Company stock holdings (see chapter 6) of the Union Pacific. Harriman as chairman of the executive committee was given discretionary power by the Union Pacific board on 5 February 1901 to use the funds provided by the sale of these bonds, "as in his judgment may be practicable and desirable."[1] The convertible bonds were quickly taken up in the market. At the time their purchase was somewhat speculative since the security behind them was at the moment inadequate. The security was 1,135 miles of improved railroad and a collateral lien on securities of the Oregon Short Line and the Oregon Railroad & Navigation Company with par value (but certainly not market value) of $66 million—which securities were held as free assets in the treasury of the Union Pacific. The sweeping success of the Union Pacific (and Southern Pacific) reconstruction and Harriman's management made this a very remunerative gamble indeed. By 1906 when the conversion privilege on the 1901 Union Pacific bonds expired (and virtually all the bonds had long since been converted) every holder of a $1,000 bond could have received in its stead ten shares of Union Pacific common, salable in the open market for $1,565. Moreover, the common stock dividend was 4.5 percent in 1905 and 5.5 in 1906. Again, those investors who hitched their hopes for profit to Harriman's star were amply rewarded.

At the time that Harriman and his associates gained control, the Southern Pacific was the largest transportation system under one ownership in the world. Its almost nine thousand miles of track ran in eight states or territories. By way of San Francisco, Los Angeles, Yuma, and El Paso it operated a continuous main line (the Sunset Route) from Portland, Oregon, to New Orleans. The Central Pacific provided a second transcontinental track from San Francisco to Ogden. The main lines were supported by extensive feeders including a substantial connection into Mexico. The hinterland of this system comprises about one-third of the geographic area of the United States. It was, of course, a much smaller portion of the economy, but still a very significant fraction. In addition to the railroads, the Southern Pacific Company reached beyond the continental United States with steamship lines connecting its eastern terminus with Havana and New York and the West with Yokohama, Shanghai, and other important parts of the Orient. River steamers, passenger ferries, and tugs were also operated by the Southern Pacific Company.

The Southern Pacific had a large and diversified traffic. To a greater extent than the Union Pacific, the Southern Pacific's business and profit derived from local traffic of the area tributary to its far-flung system of feeder lines. In 1901 gross revenues of the Southern Pacific Company were $77.7 million or almost 79 percent larger than the Union Pacific.

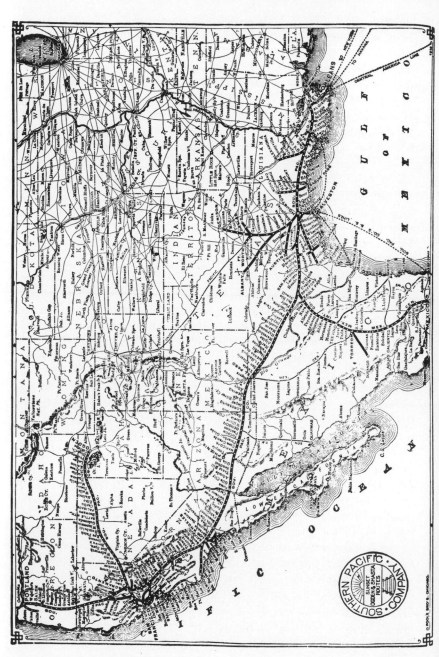

Capital earnings of the Southern Pacific in that year were only 40 percent larger than the Union Pacific so its margin of gross revenue to operating expenses was significantly less than the Union Pacific's. The funded debt was huge: $350 million, and the Southern Pacific Company had never paid a dividend. Even if reconstruction of the Central Pacific were not necessary, here was a worthy challenge for Harriman's talents. The potential profit to be reaped from application of the management skills he had honed at the Illinois Central and the Union Pacific was substantial.

Reconstruction

Compared to other western roads the Southern Pacific Company lines were not in bad shape. However, they were significantly below the standard set by the reconstructed Union Pacific. About two-thirds of the road had rails of only 60 pounds to the yard and only about one-tenth had rails of 75 pounds or more. Two hundred miles of trestles and bridges were still of timber. Grades of 45 to 90 feet per mile were frequent between Ogden and Reno. Also in this section of the Central Pacific, curves were so numerous and sharp that the road made thirty-six complete circles in that stretch alone. Improvement here was crucial. The Central Pacific had to be able to move as much freight from Ogden to San Francisco as the Union Pacific could move from Ogden to Omaha. In 1901 this was not the case.

The virtual reconstruction of the Central Pacific was budgeted for $18 million and was under the direct supervision of Julius Kruttschnitt, the general manager of the Southern Pacific System and a railroad engineer. The work took a little under three years. It required the abandonment of 373 miles of the old road and replacement of these with 322 miles of new. The new road was fifty miles shorter, had thirteen thousand less degrees of curvature, and maximum grades were reduced from 49 to 90 feet per mile to 21 feet per mile. On the old line many curves were 8 and 10 degrees while on the new line the maximum was less than 4 degrees. About three thousand vertical feet were saved in grade, the equivalent of a continuous grade of 50 feet per mile for sixty miles.

The construction of the Lucin cutoff across the Great Salt Lake was the most impressive engineering feat in the Central Pacific's reconstruction. The original Central Pacific was routed around the north end of the lake through very rough terrain with maximum curves of 10 degrees and grades up to 90 feet to the mile and an elevation variation from 4,200 to 4,900 feet above sea level. The idea of the cutoff was not Harriman's but that of William Hood who was Huntington's chief engineer. When it was completed on 26 November 1903, the maximum grade became 21 feet per mile instead of 90, four thousand degrees of curvature were eliminated, and the distance reduced from 147 to 103 miles. The cutoff was only three-fourths of a mile longer than the straight-line distance between its terminal points. The Lucin cutoff alone cost about $9 million. The changes described in the reconstruction of the Central Pacific made it possible (with new equipment) to bring the road's freight capacity up to the level of the rebuilt Union Pacific and thus allowed the full benefits of the latter investment to be reaped.

The engineering difficulties in reconstruction of the Southern Pacific main line between San Francisco and New Orleans were much less than those encountered on the Central Pacific. Extensive betterments including heavier rails, new crossties, better ballast, and stronger culverts and bridges were required.

Two cutoffs were constructed on the main line. The Bay Shore cutoff substantially improved the approach into San Francisco. The old road had been built in 1863 and ran into the city on the west side of San Bruno Mountain. From San Bruno to the terminal the old road was eleven miles long and in that distance had 796 degrees of curvature and a maximum grade of 158 feet to the mile. In forty years the city had grown up around the railroad so that it was virtually impossible to correct the existing road. Consequently a new double-track line was built on the east side of San Bruno Mountain along the shore of San Francisco Bay. The new road saved 2.65 miles in length, eliminated 592 degrees of curvature, lowered the maximum elevation from 292 feet to 20 feet, and brought the maximum grade down to 16 feet per mile from 158 feet per mile. Altogether this was an engineering achievement second only to the Lucin cutoff. Its cost was $9.3 million.

The second cutoff on the main line (the Montalvo cutoff) was one of sixty miles in southern California on the main line between Burbank and Montalvo. Harriman's goal as in all his rebuilding was reduction of grade and elimination of curvature. The old line through Saugus had a maximum grade of 116 feet per mile. The new line through the Santa Susana tunnel was seven miles shorter, 511 feet lower in maximum elevation, had a maximum grade of 53 feet and 2,276 less degrees of curvature.

Improvements on the Southern Pacific Company roads cost about $52 million during Harriman's administration. About two-fifths of this sum was for the three cutoffs: the Lucin, Bay Shore, and Montalvo. This seems at first blush like an exorbitant amount to spend on three relatively small sections of track on nine thousand miles of railroad. However, Harriman correctly saw that these three stretches of track were binding bottlenecks on the whole system. Without their improvement, the expenditure of no sum of money on the remainder of the track would bring the Southern Pacific's freight capacity up to the standard he had set on the Union Pacific. These improvements were the crucial ingredient in Harriman's management of the Southern Pacific and the combined operation of the Union Pacific and Southern Pacific.

A lesser improvement of great value to both the railroad and society was pushed on Harriman's personal initiative. This was the installation of an excellent system of automatic block signals. In the nineteenth and early twentieth centuries railroading was a dangerous business not only for employees of the roads but also for the public, especially passengers. By 1901 very little automatic signaling had been installed. On the Southern Pacific lines only about fifty miles of block-signaled track existed in 1901. During the Harriman period this was increased to almost three thousand miles at a cost of $2.8 million. There followed a significant decline in train accidents (about 50 percent) on the Southern Pacific roads. In 1914 the American Museum of Safety awarded the Harriman gold medal to the Southern Pacific because it had the best accident prevention program and had done the most to protect passenger lives. The accident rate had been reduced by two-thirds for the Southern Pacific lines and not a single passenger had been killed in the preceding five years.

In addition to improving existing railroad Harriman also managed the construction of 1,500 miles of new railroad for the Southern Pacific Company. About eight hundred miles of this was included in the Mexican extension of the Southern Pacific, begun after Harriman's visit to Mexico and discussion with President Diaz and others in 1902. Thus, while his most important work was in improving railroads built by others so as to gain the advantages of capacity improvement in rolling stock, Harriman also found the time and money to undertake some not insignificant extensions of mileage.

Along with reconstruction of the Southern Pacific lines, Harriman sharply upgraded the rolling stock to make it possible to gain the full benefits of potential capacity and productivity improvements embodied in the reconstructed lines. Table 5–1 shows the rolling stock figures for the Southern Pacific Company in the Harriman years. As we noted in considering this topic earlier, these mere numbers are only suggestive of the capacity change brought about by rolling stock augmentation. However, in the Southern Pacific case (and somewhat surprisingly more so than for

Table 5–1
Southern Pacific Company
Rolling Stock[a]

Year	Locomotives	Passenger	Freight	Service
1901	1,282	1,250	35,476	1,738
1902	1,374	1,331	39,518	2,463
1903	1,468	1,345	44,922	3,078
1904	1,555	1,527	43,756	3,218
1905	1,703	1,576	44,801	3,267
1906	1,667	1,653	44,284	4,021
1907	1,759	1,707	43,757	4,517
1908	1,858	1,758	43,828	4,877
1909	1,837	1,771	44,578	5,398

[a]Source: Company reports in annual volumes of Poor, *Manual of Railroads.*

the Union Pacific) the numbers alone are tremendously impressive. To 1909 the mere number of locomotives increases 43 percent over 1901 while the actual capacity involved because of the addition of larger and more powerful locomotives probably more than doubles. The percentage increase in passenger cars (42 percent) is about the same as for locomotives and, while freight cars in number rose only 26 percent, capacity was probably more than doubled. The more than threefold increase in service cars bears testimony to the extent of improvement and construction activities. What we see here is ample evidence of growth in rolling stock capacity to mesh with the rise in potential capacity created by reconstruction. New equipment in the Harriman era cost about $41 million for the Southern Pacific Company.

Operation

The Southern Pacific Company of which Harriman gained control in 1901 was quite a different proposition from the reorganized Union Pacific in 1898. The Southern Pacific Company had never seen the abyss of insolvency. Gross revenues of the company declined about 11 percent in the hard times between 1892 and 1894 (from $50.4 million to $44.8 million) but then rebounded much more strongly than those of the Union Pacific, rising to $75.6 million (an increase of 69 percent) in 1900. Over the whole period (1889–1900) gross revenues of the Southern Pacific rose 63 percent. The record for capital earnings (revenue minus variable operating costs) was similar although the hard times fall was greater. During the economic downturn between 1892 and 1894 capital earnings of the Southern Pacific declined almost 22 percent (from $18.0 million to $14.1 million) but then recovered even more sharply to $26.4 million in 1900 (a rise of 87 percent over 1894).

The years of Harriman management saw a further comfortable rise in both gross revenues (from $80.4 million in 1901 to $120.5 million in 1909 or a 50 percent increase) and capital earnings (from $26.6 million in 1901 to $40.9 million in 1909, a rise of 57 percent). *Historical Statistics of the United States* shows revenue rising about as fast for all U. S. roads, but capital earnings rising significantly slower: 47 percent between 1901 and 1909. A major factor in the more rapid rise of capital earnings compared to the earlier period and all U. S. roads during the years of Harriman's control is the benefit derived from the reconstruction and reequipment of the Southern Pacific Company lines. Between 1889 and 1900 both gross revenues and operating expenses rose slightly less than gross revenues: 48 percent versus 50 percent. While this is a small difference, it translates into over $1 million in 1909. Moreover, without the Harriman improvements the rise in operating costs to handle the 1909 volume of business would have been significantly more than the actual rise.

Table 5–2 lists the investment costs and capital earnings of the Southern Pacific Company for 1889–1909 in real terms. The capital stock value of the Atlantic Division included in the 1889 investment cost is estimated by the 75-10 rule, i.e., 75 percent of the value of the funded debt plus 10 percent of the value of capital stock. This leads to an 1889 estimated capital value per mile for these roads of $20,605 compared to $22,007 for the Pacific Division. Considering terrain, etc., we would expect the Pacific Division to be somewhat higher. The book value per mile of road and equipment for the Atlantic Division roads is $52,030 which is clearly substantially inflated. Several roads were added to the Atlantic Division in the nineties and their estimated capital stock is included in the investment costs in Table 5–2 using the Pacific Division capital value per mile.

The internal rate of return is calculated from 1889–1900 and for 1901–1909 based on the data of Table 5–2. The Southern Pacific Company was quite profitable in both periods, with an internal rate of return of 11.6

Table 5–2
Southern Pacific Company
Investment Costs and Capital Earnings[a]

Year	Investment Costs (000 1900$)	Capital Earnings (000 1900$)
1889	134,076[b]	14,970
1890	3,810	15,970
1891	4,477	17,998
1892	4,058	16,517
1893	2,273	16,925
1894	1,473	16,540
1895	6,390	18,270
1896	18,228	18,389
1897	1,513	18,585
1898	7,689	21,119
1899	12,030	22,379
1900	13,413	26,359
1901	156,855[c]	26,942
1902	11,570	25,488
1903	17,179	24,396
1904	16,487	25,753
1905	11,895	27,583
1906	10,947	31,803
1907	8,373	37,085
1908	6,604	30,935
1909	10,950	33,973

[a]Underlying data from company reports in annual volumes of Poor, *Manual of Railroads.*

[b]Includes 1889 capital stock value of the Pacific Division from Lloyd J. Mercer, *Railroads and Land Grant Policy: A Study in Government Intervention* (New York: Academic Press, 1982, p. 260 and the estimated capital stock value of the Atlantic Division discussed in the text.

[c]Includes capital stock estimate.

percent for the former and 15.4 percent for the Harriman years. By this measure the results of Harriman's management are again evident. Despite an investment expenditure of just over $110 million the internal rate of return for the Harriman period is about one-third higher than that of the preceding one.

The gross accounting rates of return in Table 5–3 give another measure of Southern Pacific profitability in the two periods. The mean gross accounting rate of return in the first period is very close to the economic (internal) rate of return, 11.44 versus 11.6. For the Harriman period the gross accounting rate of return is less than the economic (internal) rate of return (10.93 compared to 15.4) and less than that of the earlier period. The reason for this anomalous result is the very substantial investment of the Harriman period coupled with the price level movements which, with this accounting technique, pulls the annual rates and the mean rate of re-

Table 5–3
Southern Pacific Company
Gross Accounting Rates of Return

Year	Gross Capital (000 1900$)	Capital Earnings (000 1900$)	Gross Accounting Rate of Return (%)
1889	134,976	14,970	11.17
1890	137,886	15,928	11.55
1891	142,363	17,998	12.64
1892	146,421	16,517	11.28
1893	148,694	16,925	11.38
1894	150,167	16,540	11.01
1895	156,557	18,270	11.67
1896	174,785	18,389	10.52
1897	176,298	18,585	10.54
1898	183,987	21,119	11.49
1899	196,017	22,379	11.42
1900	209,430	26,359	12.59
		Mean rate	11.44
1901	216,522	26,492	12.24
1902	228,092	25,488	11.17
1903	245,271	24,396	9.95
1904	261,758	25,753	9.84
1905	273,653	27,583	10.08
1906	284,600	31,803	11.17
1907	292,973	37,085	12.66
1908	299,576	30,935	10.33
1909	310,526	33,973	10.94
		Mean rate	10.93

turn down. Between end points, the gross capital grew 43 percent in the Harriman years while real capital earnings increased only 26 percent. For the earlier period, real gross capital rose 56 percent and real capital earnings climbed 76 percent. Because the economic (interal) rate of return is the superior measure of profitability, our conclusion that Harriman significantly increased the profitability of the Southern Pacific Company holds despite these perverse results with the gross accounting rate of return.

Another means of examining the consequences of Harriman's management of the Southern Pacific Company is provided by the movement in productivity given by changes in passenger miles per mile of road and freight ton miles per mile of road. Table 5–4 provides the relevant information for that evaluation. For passenger output per mile of road we see a steep increase in the Harriman years (56 percent in eight years) compared with the earlier period (13 percent in eleven years). The substantial increase during the last four years of the 1899–1900 period results is a sharp rise in freight output per mile (114 percent over eleven years) for the period. Prior to this surge, the increase is only about one-third in eight years. During the Harriman era the rise is less (45 percent to the 1907 peak), but the period is shorter (only six years to the 1907 peak). The rise in freight output per mile is half again as fast as for all U. S. railroads over the 1901–1907 period (45 percent versus 30 percent). Moreover, freight output per mile is 18 percent above the figure for all U. S. roads in 1907 (850.54 as compared to 721.40 in thousands of ton miles per mile). This compares with only 6 percent above the U. S. average in 1901 when Harriman gained control of the Southern Pacific (587.43 as against 554.27 in thousands of ton miles per mile). While the margin is not so great as in the Union Pacific case, the consequence of Harriman management of the Southern Pacific was to benefit the users of the railroad's services as productivity was significantly increased.

Average passenger and freight rates for the Southern Pacific for 1899–1909 are shown in Table 5–5. Between 1901 and 1909 the average passenger rate declined 22 percent for the Southern Pacific Company. The decline is slightly larger than that for the Union Pacific for the comparable period and the 1909 rate a little under the average for the Union Pacific.

For freight the Southern Pacific record diverges from the other Harriman roads. The nominal freight rate actually increases 15 percent between 1901 and 1909. The real freight rate declines, but only by 6

Table 5–4
Southern Pacific Company
Passenger and Freight Output Per Mile of Road[a]

Year	Passenger Miles (000 per mile of road)	Freight Ton Miles (000 per mile of road)
1889	78.90	290.80
1890	74.39	330.35
1891	74.47	321.74
1892	73.86	318.41
1893	70.76	353.53
1894	67.95	372.53
1895	59.03	371.14
1896	66.15	355.37
1897	63.39	393.55
1898	76.97	506.87
1899	74.96	551.60
1900	89.44	621.44
1901	90.92	587.43
1902	105.91	692.00
1903	115.41	713.47
1904	123.85	727.40
1905	126.46	718.36
1906	134.88	787.29
1907	147.52	850.54
1908	152.76	825.27
1909	142.00	749.43

[a]Data source is the company reports in the annual volumes of Poor, *Manual of Railroads.*

percent. While the Southern Pacific average passenger rate is only 13 percent above the 1909 average for all U. S. roads, the freight rate is 50 percent higher. This higher rate is undoubtedly in part a product of the Southern Pacific's lower traffic density than the average for all U. S. roads. Some significant part of the higher rate is surely due to the lack of competition in a major portion of the Southern Pacific's market. This is true of passenger traffic as well as freight traffic but does not show up to the same extent for passenger traffic. The result is some diminution of

Table 5–5
Southern Pacific Company
Average Passenger and Freight Rates[a]

Year	Average Passenger Rates[b] per mile		Average Freight Rates[c] per ton mile	
	actual	1900 = 100[d]	actual	1900 = 100[d]
	(cents)		(cents)	
1899	2.25	2.42	0.95	1.02
1900	2.18	2.18	0.98	0.98
1901	2.28	2.31	1.00	1.01
1902	2.20	2.10	1.02	0.97
1903	2.18	2.05	1.02	0.96
1904	2.14	2.01	1.01	0.95
1905	2.18	2.04	1.05	0.98
1906	2.24	2.03	1.02	0.93
1907	2.11	1.82	1.10	0.95
1908	2.17	1.94	1.10	0.98
1909	2.18	1.81	1.15	0.95

[a]Source: Annual volumes of Poor, *Manual of Railroads.*
[b]Revenue per passenger mile.
[c]Revenue per freight ton mile.
[d]Based on Bureau of Labor Statistics Wholesale Price Index from *Historical Statistics of the United States* with 1900 set equal to 100.

the benefit of Harriman's productivity improvement of the Southern Pacific for the public.

Table 5–6 presents a comparison of real passenger rates for the Southern Pacific (and Union Pacific) and several major eastern and western roads for 1899–1909. The same information for freight rates is shown in Table 5–7. As to passenger rates, the Union Pacific is the lowest of the western roads in 1909 while the Southern Pacific is the third lowest of five roads. The Santa Fe and Northern Pacific show slightly faster declines over the period. The Southern Pacific has the least decline of the roads shown.

In freight rates the Union Pacific is the third lowest of the western roads and the Southern Pacific the most expensive. It appears that this ranking is primarily the result of relative traffic density and mix. The decline in freight rates is faster for the Union Pacific (and slower for the Southern Pacific) than the average for the roads shown.

Table 5–6
Revenue Per Passenger Mile (1900$)
(cents)

Year	New York Central	Pennsylvania	Chicago, Burlington & Quincy	Baltimore & Ohio	Santa Fe	Great Northern	Northern Pacific	Union Pacific	Southern Pacific
1899	1.90	2.09	2.25	1.87	2.38	2.29	2.46	2.09	2.10
1900	1.80	1.96	2.18	1.82	2.21	2.33	2.35	1.97	1.93
1901	1.83	2.02	2.20	2.01	2.29	2.26	2.31	2.12	2.01
1902	1.64	1.91	2.03	1.92	2.11	2.18	2.08	1.92	1.83
1903	1.67	1.90	1.96	1.88	2.07	2.18	2.03	1.83	1.78
1904	1.66	1.90	1.99	1.88	2.03	2.22	2.08	1.80	1.79
1905	1.62	1.88	1.83	1.83	2.02	2.23	2.09	2.01	2.04
1906	1.59	1.84	1.86	1.82	1.90	2.12	1.90	1.69	1.86
1907	1.50	1.70	1.78	1.69	1.85	2.03	1.95	1.69	1.85
1908	1.54	1.71	1.65	1.69	1.85	2.03	2.04	1.74	1.98
1909	1.45	1.60	1.54	1.57	1.66	1.86	1.88	1.63	1.81
1909/1899	0.763	0.766	0.684	0.84	0.70	0.81	0.76	0.78	0.86

Source: Nominal rates from *Report on the Statistics of Railways in the United States.* Conversion to real rates performed in the same fashion as before.

Table 5–7
Revenue Per Freight Ton Mile (1900$)
(cents)

Year	New York Central	Pennsylvania	Chicago, Burlington & Quincy	Baltimore & Ohio	Santa Fe	Great Northern	Northern Pacific	Union Pacific	Southern Pacific
1899	0.63	0.50	0.98	0.42	1.03	1.05	1.13	1.09	1.05
1900	0.56	0.51	0.98	0.46	0.95	0.96	0.99	1.05	0.93
1901	0.58	0.58	0.88	0.51	0.95	0.94	0.96	1.06	0.95
1902	0.58	0.56	0.85	0.49	0.88	0.87	0.86	0.93	0.88
1903	0.60	0.56	0.82	0.52	0.85	0.80	0.81	0.92	0.84
1904	0.63	0.57	0.81	0.55	0.92	0.84	0.83	0.92	0.85
1905	0.57	0.55	0.79	0.53	0.94	0.75	0.78	0.84	0.99
1906	0.57	0.53	0.73	0.56	0.82	0.71	0.75	0.84	1.00
1907	0.55	0.51	0.68	0.54	0.80	0.65	0.69	0.83	1.00
1908	0.55	0.51	0.71	0.51	0.84	0.70	0.80	0.86	1.04
1909	0.52	0.47	0.66	0.48	0.85	0.68	0.74	0.83	1.03
1909/1899	0.825	0.94	0.67	1.14	0.825	0.65	0.65	0.76	0.98

Source: Nominal rates from *Report on the Statistics of Railways in the United States*. Conversion to real rates performed in the same fashion as before.

The Monopoly Power Question

The Union Pacific–Southern Pacific de facto merger resulting from the Union Pacific's attainment of control of the management of the Southern Pacific Company certainly increased the monopoly power of the combined roads. The Harriman management controlled 19 percent of the total railroad mileage west of the Mississippi–Missouri River and south of the Northern Pacific Railroad. It controlled two of the major transcontinental tracks in that region, but its transcontinental monopoly power was moderated by the Atchison, Topeka & Santa Fe which offered a third alternative. Harriman in 1904 offered to exchange two seats on the Southern Pacific board for two on the Santa Fe board. This was rejected, but he and his associates then bought 300,000 shares of Santa Fe stock which allowed them to elect two directors to the Santa Fe board to represent the interests of the Union Pacific and Southern Pacific. In this way undoubtedly some moderating influence was brought to bear on the transcontinental competition provided by the Santa Fe. What Harriman and many others (including J. P. Morgan) would have called a community of interest was established.

Harriman's position on the question of community of interest is well illustrated by a speech he gave at the St. Louis Exposition in 1904. The topic of the speech was cooperation and his point was that human endeavor depended on and succeeded only because of cooperation. What he had to say about railroad combinations and the law in this speech undoubtedly represents the basis from which he operated. He said:

The combination of different railways should be regulated by law. So far as may be necessary the public interest should be protected by law, but in so far as the law obstructs such combinations, without public benefit, it is unwise and prejudiced to the public interest.[2]

Public and court hostility toward big business did not seem paramount in 1901 when control of the Southern Pacific was acquired. Both increased over time. In 1908 the federal government attacked the Union Pacific–Southern Pacific consolidation as a combination in restraint of trade under the provisions of the Sherman Anti-Trust Act of 1890.

Harriman's primary motive in acquisition of the Southern Pacific appears to have been the necessity to rebuild the Central Pacific so as to gain the full benefit from his reconstruction and reequipment of the Union Pacific and the resultant substantial increase in its capacity. At the same time, a powerful secondary motive must have been to get the Union Pacific out of the competitive bind in which it found itself with regard to transcontinental traffic. The Central Pacific provided an important part of the Union Pacific's transcontinental traffic, but its owners controlled an alternative transcontinental route, the Sunset Route. Thus, the Harriman purchase of control of the Southern Pacific Company accomplished two important objectives from the point of view of the Union Pacific. First, it made it possible to fully achieve the productivity gains built into the revitalized Union Pacific. Second, the Union Pacific would no longer be at the mercy of a transcontinental competitor with regard to a significant part of its own transcontinental traffic.

Counsel for the Union Pacific in 1911 made two main arguments against the goverment's case. One was that the consolidation of the two roads did not run afoul of the Sherman Act because the roads had not competed prior to the consolidation. The second was that the government could not interfere because the consolidation occurred as a result of stock purchases rather than contract or agreement between the corporations.

The government, in contradiction, presented an elaborate analysis of the competitive relations between the Southern Pacific and Union Pacific. The government insisted that the Central and Southern Pacific continuously diverted all the traffic they could to the Sunset Route before 1901. The reason for this is obvious, namely, the Southern Pacific received all revenue over the latter route, but only 30.1 percent of transcontinental revenue for freight over the Central Pacific. The goverment was able to demonstrate to the court's satisfaction the existence of competition before 1901 and its cessation afterward. On this basis the government eventually won its case in the Supreme Court and forced the Union Pacific to divest itself of its Southern Pacific stock which it did under a reorganization plan of May 1913.

The profitability and productivity gains of the Union Pacific under Harriman were undoubtedly greater than they would have been in the absence of control of the Southern Pacific Company. The change in competitive environment undoubtedly redounded to the advantage of the Union Pacific. This was by itself, however, probably not a significant part of the gain in profitability and productivity that we earlier attributed to Harriman's management. In any event, whatever gain occurred is simply another product of Harriman's management, in this case the result of the acquisition of control of the Southern Pacific. The government did not show in its elaborate analysis that the roads involved had raised or held up rates, or engaged in some nefarious discrimination. What was demonstrated was in essence a technical violation of the Sherman Act creating some *potential* to raise prices (or retard their decline) or discriminate or whatever. There is no evidence available nor was any such evidence presented by the government showing that this potential was realized, creating any adverse impact on society. The net impact of Harriman's Southern Pacific management was positive: for his associates and investors, and for society.

CHAPTER SIX

Captain of Finance: The Northern Securities Company and Its Aftermath

The Battle for the Burlington

As we have seen, Harriman was extremely successful as a railroad manager and operator. In part, even to have the opportunity to exercise these skills he also had to be an intelligent and successful railroad financier. His actions in that role have drawn more attention and attack both contemporaneously and by later commentators than his operating and management activities. Our examination of Harriman's activities in the field of railroad finance will focus on the Northern Securities Company and its aftermath and the Chicago Alton.

The region west of the Mississippi River was one of the areas of greatest growth in the United States in the later nineteenth century. Along with the region's rapid economic growth there also occurred a swift expansion of its transportation business, especially the railroad business. The growth of interregional trade between the West and the remainder of the country was particularly impressive. While there were other major systems including the Chicago, Milwaukee & St. Paul, the Chicago & Northwestern, and the Rock Island, the transportation market of the American West by the final two decades of the nineteenth century was dominated by five railroad systems. These were the Great Northern; the Northern Pacific; the Chicago, Burlington & Quincy; the Union Pacific;

and the Southern Pacific. In the Northwest the Great Northern and the Northern Pacific largely complemented each other in the agricultural, manufacturing, and mining hinterlands. However, these two great systems did not have direct connection with Chicago. The Burlington did have such a connection along with an interface with the major cities of the Midwest and even west to Omaha and Denver. The more southerly systems, the Union Pacific and the Southern Pacific, were of course in competition with their northern brethren for the interregional trade of the West. Moreover, by 1901 the two southerly systems had come under control of a single interest, Harriman and his associates. Thus, the stage was set for one of the titanic financial battles of American railroad history: the struggle for control of the Burlington and its midwestern and Chicago interface.

By 1900 both the Great Northern and the Northern Pacific interests had developed a strong desire to expand eastward to the Midwest and Chicago. Construction of a new line was one possibility to achieve this goal, but it was not very attractive by the 1890s because it would involve considerable duplication and waste of resources. Far more appealing was the lease or purchase of an existing railroad. Five different lines comprised the feasible set for such a move. These included: the Wisconsin Central; Chicago & Northwestern; Chicago, Milwaukee & St. Paul; Chicago, Burlington & Quincy; and the Chicago Great Western. Because the routes into Chicago of the Wisconsin Central and the Chicago Great Western were somewhat indirect and because their feederline networks were less well developed, the other three railroads appear to be the only ones seriously considered.

The testimony in the Northern Securities case itself does not reveal the relative ranking of these possibilities in the eyes of the Great Northern and the Northern Pacific interests. However, the preferences of J. J. Hill and his banker, J. P. Morgan, are known from other sources. Their preferences did not coincide in the early exploratory negotiations. Morgan preferred the Chicago, Milwaukee & St. Paul because he judged the financial responsibility less with that road and he wanted to ensure that it would not build to the West Coast. Hill's preference was the Burlington because of its traffic possibilities and its line to Billings, Montana. Hill also recognized that the Burlington was a better-built and better-run road. He had discussed its acquisition with London financiers as early as 1897. An extraneous factor was significant in making the Burlington the leading acquisition choice for both Hill and Morgan. This was the purchase of the Burlington stock available on the open market by Union Pacific interests. The choice was sealed by the fact that Morgan's approach to the directors of the Milwaukee regarding terms for sale of their road was firmly rejected. The Milwaukee directors would not state terms for a sale.

The Union Pacific (Harriman) became interested in the Burlington because of its Chicago connection, its close competition with the Union Pacific east of Denver including a line roughly paralleling the Oregon Short Line, and the possibility that the Burlington could extend its main line from Denver to the Pacific, becoming a transcontinental competitor for the Harriman lines (the Union Pacific and Southern Pacific). Control of the line paralleling the Oregon Short Line was probably the major consideration. The possibility that the Burlington would extend its main line to the Pacific seemed unlikely to be realized for the same reasons that the Northern Pacific and the Great Northern did not seriously contemplate construction as the means for entrance to Chicago. A persistent rumor was that the Pennsylvania Railroad would come to the aid of the Burlington in building its own line from Denver to the Pacific. Even if a westward move by the Burlington was unlikely, the first two points by themselves and especially the competition with the Oregon Short Line provide ample reason for Harriman to interest himself in control of the Burlington.

The Burlington by 1901 was no small fry in the railroad pond. Its eastern terminus was Chicago, its farthest cast west was Denver. It closely paralleled the Union Pacific between Denver and the Missouri River with a close-knit network of feeder lines in Kansas, Nebraska, and Colorado. These carried a substantial volume of freight (and passengers) originating in or destined for territory the Union Pacific had come to consider its own. In addition, the Burlington ran to St. Paul, St. Louis, and Kansas City with good terminals and connections, and had a network of lines in northern Illinois as well as southern Iowa and northern Missouri. The line built in the 1880s and 1890s from the Burlington's Nebraska heartland to a Northern Pacific connection at Billings, Montana, gave the Burlington its own western outlet and provided a third northwestern transcontinental route alternative to the Union Pacific. Exclusive of leased and controlled roads, the Burlington of 1901 operated 7,911 miles of railroad that were well constructed and managed and quite profitable. Here indeed was a nontrivial competitive force in the Union Pacific's market and a prize worthy of Harriman's vision and grasp. J. J. Hill and J. P. Morgan were also not lacking in either vision or acquisitiveness and the Burlington was a tempting a prize to them. The luster of this ''money machine'' was not diminished to Hill and Morgan by the possibility that it might easily fall into Harriman's control. Thus, the Union Pacific nibbles in the market in late 1900 and early 1901 powerfully focused the attention of the Northern Pacific and Great Northern interests on the Burlington.

The Union Pacific's competition with the Northern Pacific and the Great Northern was by 1901 focused on the Burlington and the entrance into Chicago. Earlier this competition had a more western flavor. In 1897 Charles E. Perkins, president of the Burlington, had written:

The key to the Pacific Railroad situation is control of the Oregon Short Line. Anyone owning the majority of its stock can do more to keep peace west of the Missouri River than all other influences put together.[1]

The Oregon Railway & Navigation Company was also in Perkins's mind (and in others') in 1897 for good reason. The western rivalry of the Union Pacific, the Northern Pacific, and the Great Northern focused on the two Oregon roads, especially the Oregon Railway & Navigation Company. In the 1880s the Union Pacific had become a transcontinental road and escaped the vice in which it found itself between the Central Pacific and the Southern Pacific by building the Oregon Short Line. Its connection to the coast and the ports of Portland and Seattle rested on movement over the Oregon Railway & Navigation Company. When the reorganized Union Pacific in 1899 gained control of the Oregon Railway & Navigation Company, it became a northwestern transcontinental in direct competition with the Northern Pacific and the Great Northern. Acquisition of the Burlington by either side in 1901 would have a tremendous impact on the competitive balance among the three transcontinentals.

The Union Pacific's initial forays in the open market for Burlington stock did not produce anything approaching control. The main result was to alert the competition and to unite the Northern Pacific and the Great Northern interests. The difficulty with the open market route was that much of the Burlington stock had been long held by people who had inherited it. As Albro Martin succinctly puts it, ''The Burlington was one of the most widely held widows-and-orphans securities in the western world.''[2] Buying control of the Burlington in the open market at par or even a price fairly significantly above par was an impossible task.

Of the potential suitors, Harriman was the first to enter into direct negotiations with the Burlington. In 1899 he suggested the Union Pacific purchase of the Burlington to George B. Harris, the second vice-president and general manager. Five conferences with Perkins followed in early 1900. Harriman offered to pay $200 a share in Union Pacific 3 percent bonds or alternatively $140 in cash, but Perkins adamantly held out for $200 a share in cash. Harriman considered this an impossible figure and formed a syndicate with Jacob Schiff of Kuhn, Loeb & Company, James Stillman of the National City Bank, and George J. Gould to purchase Burlington stock. Sales of Burlington stock increased sharply and its price rose from $124 in January to $131 in June while the syndicate acquired 70,000 shares. By the end of July the syndicate ceased its open market effort after having obtained 80,300 shares, less than 9 percent of the 984,461 shares outstanding. Harriman's proposal for the Burlington and the Union Pacific to share directors was rejected and in November and December 1900 his syndicate sold 40,300 of their shares at prices between $130 and $140.

The next move in the contest for the Burlington was undertaken by Hill and Morgan. The surprising thing is that Harriman apparently did not actively interfere in his rivals' efforts. Harriman's biographer, George Kennan, writes that the reason for this uncharacteristic position on Harriman's part was his deep involvement in the ongoing reconstruction of the Union Pacific and the Southern Pacific. The price of Burlington stock rose to 148-1/2 with over 200,000 shares traded in January 101. One or more serious bids for control were apparently underway. Hill and Perkins had a number of meetings in the first months of 1901, Perkins stubbornly holding to his price of $200 per share in cash. In the end, in meetings started 7 March and continuing to 9 April, Perkins insisted on a minimum price of 4 percent bonds (up from the 3.5 percent bonds Hill offered earlier) at $200 per share or the cash alternative of $200 per share. Following Hill's capitulation, Perkins issued a call for the stock to be sold and 97 percent of it was presented. The Northern Pacific and the Great Northern had won the battle for the Burlington. But the war was not over.

The Northern Securities Company

Harriman and Schiff urged Hill to give them a one-third interest in the Burlington for which they offered one-third of the purchase price. Hill rejected this offer since it would be contrary to his own ends and because he had doubts about the legality of any merger involving the parallel lines of the Burlington and the Union Pacific. The latter was also a factor in Perkins's preference for the Northern Pacific and Great Northern over the Union Pacific. Flushed with victory, Hill and Morgan departed the financial center. Morgan sailed for Italy while Hill went to the Pacific Coast to attend to business there.

Having lost the battle for the Burlington, Harriman quickly devised a strategem to reverse the tables on his competitors. In the words of an earlier biographer of Hill, Harriman's counter-move was so "daring" in conception and so "swift and unsparing in execution" as to "command admiration from friend and foe."[3] The Great Northern and the Northern Pacific now each had a half interest in the Burlington. Harriman's tactic was the purchase on the open market of a majority interest in the Northern Pacific, gaining as a result a half interest in the Burlington.

Since its reorganization in 1896 the Northern Pacific had $80 million (par value) outstanding in common stock and $75 million (par value) in preferred stock. The frantic struggle in the stock exchange for Northern Pacific stock focused on the common stock because of a provision in the articles of reorganization. That provision allowed the common stockholders to vote the retirement of the preferred stock on any 1 January to 1917. Kuhn, Loeb & Company carried out the stock purchase campaign on behalf of Harriman and Schiff. By the middle of April 1901 about 150,000 shares of common and 100,000 shares of preferred had been obtained. In early April Northern Pacific shares sold for 102 for common and 101 for preferred. At the close of business on 8 May Northern Pacific stock was up to 180.

The Northern Pacific and Hill's friends were seemingly as unaware of Harriman's counterattack as Harriman had earlier apparently been oblivious to Hill and Morgan's maneuvers to close the Burlington purchase. The Northern Pacific, tempted by the higher prices, even sold its own stock. On 2 May a subsidiary of the Northern Pacific by direction of the Northern Pacific board sold 13,000 shares, while on the same day J. P. Morgan & Company sold 10,000 shares. Most of this stock ended up in the hands of Kuhn, Loeb & Company and thus Harriman and the Union Pacific.

During the last days of the purchase campaign, as Northern Pacific prices rose rapidly, many brokers sold stock that they did not have, confident that prices would decline and they could rap a tidy profit buying stock for delivery at the lower prices. On 9 May the realization sank in that this happy scenario was not to occur. Northern Pacific stock soared over 700 and it is said that at least three shares traded at $1000. Kuhn, Loeb & Company and J. P. Morgan & Company had bought most of the stock sold by "shorts." Further disaster on the stock market was averted on 9 May by an agreement between Schiff of Kuhn, Loeb & Company and Robert Bacon of J. P. Morgan to settle with the "shorts" for $150 a share. This agreement was accepted by the "shorts." It relieved the corner in the market and restored something approaching normalcy.

The corner on Northern Pacific stock resulted not as one might at first suppose from the action of the Harriman interests, but the conditions for it were created by the counteraction of the Hill and Morgan interests, specifically from the purchase of 150,000 shares of Northern Pacific common by J. P. Morgan and Company on 6 and 7 May. This purchase was authorized by a cable to Robert Bacon from J. P. Morgan on 5 May. Hill in St. Paul, after a quick trip to Seattle at the end of April, became alarmed on April 26 at the activity in Northern Pacific stock and had rushed to New York, arriving in the morning of 29 April. A discussion with Schiff revealed what was going on and Hill cabled Morgan for authority to purchase at least 150,000 shares of Northern Pacific common stock after the close of business on 4 May. With the pressure of the Morgan purchases, Northern Pacific stock advanced from 110 to 130 on Monday, 6 May, and common reached 149-3/4 the next day. Morgan and Company made no purchases after 7 May. The further run-up of prices on 8 May and the panic of 9 May resulted from continued speculation by the general public in a market where the supply of available Northern Pacific stock was virtually zero as a result of the purchases of the contending interests.

By the close of the stock market on 3 May Kuhn, Loeb & Company had gathered a little over 370,000 shares of Northern Pacific common and about 420,000 shares of preferred. These holdings of around $79 million (par value) represented a majority of the total Northern Pacific stock but was short of a majority of the common by 30,000 to 40,000 shares. Harriman on the morning of 4 May was ill at his home and concerned about the shortfall in common for a majority holding in that class of Northern Pacific stock. He gave one of the Kuhn, Loeb & Company partners (Heinsheimer) an order to purchase 40,000 shares of Northern Pacific common, and with the substantial trading in the stock that day believed that he had attained absolute control of the Northern Pacific. Not having received the report of the execution of his Saturday order, Harriman inquired about it on Monday and discovered that Schiff had countermanded his order. Schiff (and James Stillman) believed that having a clear majority of all shares of Northern Pacific stock made it unnecessary and wasteful to buy more. This turned out to be a significant error: those 40,000 shares were the missing nail that cost Harriman this particular kingdom.

When the Northern Pacific panic was over on 9 May, the Union Pacific interests owned 781,080 shares of Northern Pacific stock which was about 6,000 shares more than half. The voting rights of the two classes of stock were equal so at the next election Harriman could choose a majority of the board of directors. however, he had lost the contest for control of the common and it was not certain that retirement of the preferred shares could be averted. If not, his control would be ephemeral.

Costly and lengthy litigation was not in the best interest of any of the parties. Moreover, the hostilities themselves had been very costly, with millions of dollars spent to gain control through stock purchases. The solution was a compromise that Morgan brought about with one of his conferences. An agreement signed on 31 May empowered Morgan to fill any vacancies on the Northern Pacific board and assured Harriman and some of his associates—Schiff, Gould, and Twombly (a Vanderbilt son-in-law)—places on the Burlington board to which they were elected in November 1901. Harriman, Twombly, and Stillman also received places on the Northern Pacific board.

To preempt reruns of the Northern Pacific struggle, Hill decided on the formation of a giant holding company as a safe haven for the securities of the Great Northern, Northern Pacific, and Burlington. This company, the Northern Securities Company, was incorporated 12 November 1901 with a capitalization of $400 million. The fifteen-member board had six representatives of the Northern Pacific, four of the Great Northern, three of the Union Pacific, and two unaffiliated. Holders of Northern Pacific and Great Northern stock were invited to exchange their shares for those of the Northern Securities Company. About 76 percent of Great Northern shares and 96 percent of Northern Pacific shares were exchanged.

The formation of the Northern Securities Company was widely viewed as a means of restricting or preventing competition among the Hill and Harriman lines. The State of Minnesota brought suit against the Northern Securities Company in the United States Circuit Court of St. Paul in late February 1902. On 10 March 1902 a suit was filed against the Northern Securities Company, the Northern Pacific, and the Great Northern in the Circuit Court of Appeals by the federal government. The decisions in the two courts were almost exactly opposite. In the state case it was found that the Securities Company involved no act or contract in restraint of trade or commerce or affecting transportation rates, more than any ordinary transfer of railroad stock from one person to another. In the federal case the unanimous conclusion of the four-judge court was that the Northern Securities Company was intended to restrain commerce and establish unreasonable rates. Whether it had done so or not was immaterial according to the court; the combination gave them the power to do so and that was illegal. Both cases were appealed to the Supreme Court where the state case was dismissed 14 March 1904 for lack of jurisdiction. The federal case was decided against the Northern Securities Company by a 5 to 4 vote, the majority opinion being that the holding company was a violation of the Sherman Act. The Northern Securities Company was ordered to divest itself of Northern Pacific and Great Northern stock.

The precise means by which the divestiture was to be accomplished was an important issue to the interested parties. There were two general possibilities. First, the company could cancel its own stock and give back to each shareholder exactly what he had surrendered for the company's stock. Second, the company could distribute its assets in proportion to each shareholder's Northern Securities holdings without regard to the kinds of stock originally received from the shareholder. This latter was probably the only reasonable solution for those who had bought Northern Securities stock on the open market. Harriman and Hill had their own preferences for good reasons. Harriman wanted the first means used while Hill wanted the second. The basis for their preference was that under the first Harriman would get back a majority of the total stock of the Northern Pacific, but under the second he would end up with a minority position in both the Northern Pacific and the Great Northern and little power in either. With control of the Northern Securities board Hill, of course, got his wish and pro rata distribution of the assets was selected. Harriman took his case to court, and on appeal the Supreme Court on 6 March 1905 denied Harriman's plea and approved Hill's plan for pro rata distribution.

The Northern Securities Company then called in its shares for cancellation and gave to the holders par values of $39.27 in Northern Pacific stock and $30.17 for Great Northern stock for every share surrendered. This distribution removed the possibility of Harriman gaining control of the Northern Pacific and also appeared to damage his financial interests seriously. If he had recovered the Northern Pacific stock he originally turned in, the par value would have been over $78 million and the annual income at the current dividend rate almost $5.5 million. Under the pro rata distribution he got back shares with a par value of only $56.7 million with current dividend income of only $4 million. It appeared at this point that Harriman would be the loser on all fronts. In fact, he was eventually a very considerable winner on the financial front as a result of this transaction.

Aftermath of the Northern Securities Divestiture

The Oregon Short Line Railroad Company received title to the Northern Pacific shares and later the Northern Securities shares. The Oregon Short Line issued $61 million in purchase money certificates in payment to the Union Pacific. The reason for this transfer was apparently to avoid by technicality the laws against the combination of parallel railroad lines. The funds for the Northern Pacific stock purchase and the Southern Pacific purchase were provided by a $100 million Union Pacific bond issue in 1901 subscribed by Union Pacific shareholders. These 4 percent bonds were convertible into common stock at par until 1 May 1906. Because the common stock was paying only a 4 percent dividend, the conversion was initially not very attractive and only $12.7 million was converted by 30 June 1904. The rapid rise in Union Pacific earnings increased the potential of the conversion so that $56.1 million of the bonds were converted in the 1905 fiscal year (ending 30 June). Following the rise in the common stock dividend rate to 5 percent in October 1905 and 6 percent in April 1906, another $32.7 million of the bonds were converted so that by August 1906 only about $500,000 of the bonds were outstanding. This brilliant financial maneuver was made possible by Harriman's reconstruction and management of the Union Pacific systems and the consequent torrent of earnings.

In 1903 the Oregon Short Line issued $36 million in 4 percent and participating (collateral trust) bonds. The security pledged was the $82.5 million of Northern Securities stock. The new bond issue was given to the Union Pacific to take up the purchase money certificates cited above. Union Pacific shareholders were offered $31 million of these bonds at 90 and $5 million were sold later. The proceeds of this transaction were used to pay off $14.5 million of loans for the Northern Pacific purchase.

Pending divestiture, the Northern Securities Company could not collect dividends declared on Great Northern and Northern Pacific stock, nor could it pay dividends on its own stock. The Oregon Short Line thus had no income on the collateral to pay the interest on the "participating fours" of 1903 and had to use funds derived from other sources. This created a potential problem because eventually the Oregon Short Line would receive these dividends. An important privilege of the holders of the "participating fours" was to share in the income received upon their collateral to the extent that that income exceeded the 4 percent interest. Thus, when the Northern Securities back dividends were paid, the "participating fours" holders could demand that all of them above the 4 percent for the year involved be distributed to themselves despite the fact that part of those dividends were in reality an offset to interest paid earlier to the bondholders. To escape this trap the Oregon Short Line called the "participating fours" at 102-1/2 as permitted under the trust indenture for these bonds and issued $100 million in 4 percent refunding twenty-five-year gold bonds in late 1905. Of this issue, 42,250 shares were sold at 96 and interest or given to owners of the "participating fours" for the principal and accrued interest on their bonds. The remaining bonds of this issue were retained in the Union Pacific Railroad Company treasury. As a result of the astute financing move described, the Great Northern and Northern Pacific stock received from the divestiture of the Northern Securities Company was not bound to any existing mortgage and could be employed by Harriman as he saw fit.

The original purchase of Northern Pacific stock cost the Union Pacific about $79.5 million of which $60 million was provided by the 1901 convertible bond issue and the remainder from bank loans. About $6.3 million of this sum was recovered in the redemption of Northern Pacific preferred shares, and an additional $3.7 million was paid on the subscription for new Great Northern stock of that amount (the Union Pacific's share) made available to Great Northern stockholders in late 1905. The final cost to the Union Pacific of the Great Northern and Northern Pacific stock it held after dissolution of the Northern Securities Company was $73.2 million to which must be added the $3.7 million for new Great Northern stock for a total cost of $76.9 million.

In terms of control of those roads, Harriman ended up the loser, when all was said and done, in the Burlington and Northern Pacific struggles. However, in the final analysis he was a very big winner indeed. The eminent economist Carl Snyder quoted Thomas Woodlock, a leading railroad expert as saying that Harriman's greatest achievement was ". . . to get licked in a fight and to pull out of it with a colossal fortune as a result."[4] Harriman's success was composed of two parts, as success usually is: luck and intelligence (and hard work). The intelligence was the brilliant financing that freed the Great Northern and Northern Pacific stocks from the collateral rules usually reserved for such stock holdings in railroad financing of the period. The luck was the extraordinary boom in the stock market in late 1905 and early 1906 which carried railroad security prices to unprecedented levels and in particular the Great Northern. Notice that, perversely, Harriman was "lucky" to have lost the battle over dissolution of the Northern Securities Company. Without this defeat he would not have had the almost $25.4 million par value of Great Northern stock which he held by late 1905.

The $82.5 million of Northern Securities Company stock held by the Oregon Short Line was disposed of in the following way. First, $10 million of it was sold for $16.9 million in cash. Second, the remaining $72.5 million was transformed upon dissolution of the Northern Securities Company into $28.2 million par value of Northern Pacific stock and $21.7 million par value of Great Northern stock and $0.7 million of Northern Securities stubs. Mr. Mahl, controller of the Union Pacific system, testified at the Interstate Commerce Commission investigation of the Harriman lines regarding the disposition of the stock obtained from the Northern Securities Company. At the time of the investigation (February 1907) $24.0 million par value of Northern Pacific stock had been sold for $50.2 million: $208.70 per share, while $4.2 million par value was still held. Of the $25.4 million of Great Northern stock, $16.4 million par value had been sold for $49.8 million: $304.41 per share, while $9 million par value remained in Union Pacific hands. Because of its Great Northern stock holdings, the Union Pacific also received 90,364 shares of Great Northern ore certificates quoted at $70 to $85 per share in 1907.

The cash realization out of these transactions was $116.8 million. Given the cash cost of $76.9 million, the Union Pacific's cash profit on all these transactions was $39.99 million or about 52 percent over a five-year period. Of course, $4.2 million par value of Northern Pacific stock and $9 million par value of Great Northern stock plus the 90,364 Great Northern ore certificates were still held. The 1906 market value of these securities was about $41.7 million ($200 per share for Northern Pacific, $300 per share for Great Northern, and $70 per ore certificate) which provides an estimate of the Union Pacific's "paper" profit from the Northern Securities Company stock. The cash plus paper profit (39.9 + 41.7) totaled $81.6 million or about 106 percent of cost for the five-year period. This was indeed a colossal fortune to be reaped from "failure."

The proceeds of the stock transactions described were reinvested in several other railroads by the Union Pacific. Table 6–1 shows the investment in other railroads from 1 October 1904 through the ICC investigation of February 1907. Of the stocks listed, all were still held 30 June 1909 except for the Fresno City Railroad and the Northern Pacific. At the time of the investigation $36.4 million of the purchase price of the

Table 6–1
Railroad Stocks Acquired by Union Pacific System and Held in 1909

	1907 Par value (millions$)	Cost[a]	cost per share ($)	1909 Par value (millions$)
Union Pacific:				
Chicago & Alton	10.3	8.7	84.00	10.3
Illinois Central	18.6	32.6	175.15	22.5
Railroad Securities Co.				
Common	3.4	6.9	202.18	3.5
Preferred	1.9	1.9	101.13	1.9
St. Joseph & Grand Island				
Common	2.9			2.9
1st preferred	0.9	2.0	39.70	0.9
2nd preferred	1.2			1.2
Fresno City Railroad	0.5	0.1	21.47	0.0
Pacific Fruit Express	1.2	1.2	100.00	7.8
TOTAL	41.0	53.5	130.40	51.0
Oregon Short Line:				
Atchison Topeka & Santa Fe				
Preferred	10.0	10.4	103.95	10.0
Baltimore & Ohio				
Common	32.3	38.8	120.00	32.3
Preferred	7.2	6.7	92.50	
Chicago, Milwaukee & St. Paul				
Common	3.7	6.3	170.04	1.8[b]
Chicago & Northwestern	2.6	5.3	204.21	3.2
New York Central	14.3	19.6	137.44	14.3
Northern Pacific	0.1	0.1	100.00	0.0
TOTAL	70.2	87.2	124.19	68.8
GRAND TOTAL	111.2	140.7	126.53	119.8

[a]From testimony of Mr. Mahl as reported in Thomas Warner Mitchel, "The Growth of the Union Pacific and Its Financial Operations," *Quarterly Journal of Economics* 21 (August 1907): 603–4.
[b]Preferred substituted for common.

Baltimore & Ohio had not been paid. Thus, the securities of Table 6–1 had involved payment of $104.3 million by that date. This represents the bulk of the cash proceeds ($116.8 million) from sale of the Northern Pacific and Great Northern stock received upon dissolution of the Northern Securities Company. While $36.4 million was still owed for securities in Table 6–1, the Union Pacific also held $12.5 million cash and stock (and ore certificates) with a value of around $40 million. The 1907 dividend income from the securities of Table 6–1 was $4.7 million or $2.1 million more than the about 2.6 percent dividend the Northern Pacific and Great Northern stocks that were sold yielded on their market value in 1906. The yield on the new portfolio in 1907 was 3.6 percent on cost versus the 2.6 percent yield on the market value of Northern Pacific and Great Northern stock. This 38 percent increase in yield was certainly good financial management on Harriman's part.

While the stock purchases in no case gave the Union Pacific majority control, they were viewed with alarm by many. In addition to increasing investment income, Harriman also had in mind creation of what was called a "community of interest." The proportion of stock held in the various companies was such that it undoubtedly had some influence on traffic policy for those companies. Otto H. Kahn, a close and sympathetic associate of Harriman, felt that these stock purchases were Harriman's one serious mistake in his management of the Union Pacific. Stuart Daggett's assessment was:

So far as Union Pacific purchases have been designed to open connections or to modify competition they have had a sound foundation. So far as they have been financial operations only they are not to be commended.[5]

Harriman's management in the stock purchases certainly aimed at (and achieved) the first point cited by Daggett. On the second point it appears that in this instance Daggett is wrong. The Union Pacific had over $100 million in cash. Good management surely required investing that cash for the best return given risk. The mere fact that the Union Pacific was a railroad surely should not have tied its hands in this regard. In this, as in the business of running the railroad itself, the Harriman management succeeded admirably. Union Pacific investment income was about $3 million in 1900, had risen to $6.5 million in 1907. Our conclusion must be that in his role as railroad financier, as illustrated in the matters described in this chapter, Harriman performed brilliantly. Out of apparent defeat he reaped for himself and his stockholders a "colossal fortune." Luck played a favorable role, but it had a significant assist from the Harriman intellect and hard work.

One additional incident in Harriman's financial management which is related to the discussion of this chapter is worth comment because it incorrectly and unfairly brought public opprobrium on Harriman. This incident was the 10 percent dividend declared on Union Pacific stock August 1906. The Union Pacific had paid its first dividend in many years in October 1898 when 1.5 percent was paid on preferred stock. This was followed by a like dividend on common stock in April 1900. In succeeding years common stock dividends were increased to 4 percent, then 4.5 percent, 6 percent, and 7 percent by fiscal 1907. The earnings of the Southern Pacific had increased sufficiently to also allow the beginning of dividend payments on that stock in 1906. Harriman decided by the spring of 1906 that a large increase in the Union Pacific dividend should be made. His concern was activated by passage of the Hepburn Act. He said to one Union Pacific director that

The time has come when instead of putting most of our money back in the property, we should give a larger share to the stockholders. If we don't the government will take it away from us.[6]

At the regular meeting of the Union Pacific board on 16 August 1906 Harriman recommended a 10 percent dividend on the common stock of the Union Pacific. This dividend was approved by the board about eleven o'clock that day, but the public announcement did not occur until ten o'clock the next morning. This delay in the announcement led to charges that Harriman and the directors bought Union Pacific stock in order to profit from their advance knowledge of the substantial increase in the dividend.

Here again Harriman's associate Otto Kahn questioned the wisdom of the action. Kahn felt that the problem was not that Harriman had acted improperly, but that the action gave the *appearance* of acting improperly. Kahn believed that the appearance as well as the substance should be avoided.

At one of the hearings where he was examined, Harriman was asked if he had bought Union Pacific stock in anticipation of the 10 percent dividend. The meaning of the question was the accusation that he had unfairly used his advance knowledge of the increased dividend. When Harriman calmly answered "Yes," the examiner turned to the audience with a broad smile. He then asked Harriman when and at what prices he had bought the stock in anticipation of the increased dividend. Harriman's answer effectively deflated the examiner and his accusers. He said,

Certainly, I shall be glad to tell you. Let me think back a minute. I bought most of that stock, many thousand shares of it, in anticipation of the 10 percent dividend declared in August 1906, some eight years before, mainly in 1898, and I paid all the way from 20 to 30 for it. And I bought more of it in subsequent years, whenever prices were low, many thousand shares more; and all the time I was accumulating it I anticipated the declaration of that dividend.[7]

The 10 percent dividend rate on Union Pacific common was maintained until 1914. Even the Harriman critic, Professor William Z. Ripley, wrote,

It is not, however, the fact but rather the manner of increasing the Union Pacific dividend which is open to criticism.[8]

It is clear that Harriman did not use his knowledge of the dividend advance improperly. At the same time both Kahn and Ripley are correct that the delay in public announcement of the increase was an error of judgment. Harriman apparently delayed the announcement because some prominent directors were out of the city on August 16 and he wanted as a matter of courtesy to inform them of the decision before the public announcement. This act of courtesy cost him dearly in public opinion at a time when he could ill afford it.

CHAPTER SEVEN

Looting or Improved Management? The Chicago & Alton

The Debate: Kennan vs. Ripley

In 1906 the Interstate Commerce Commission undertook an inquiry which focused on western roads and particularly on those roads that were controlled or at some time had been controlled by E. H. Harriman. Special attention was devoted to the financial transactions of the syndicate headed by Harriman with the Chicago & Alton Railroad starting in 1899. The ICC reported in terms of sharpest condemnation regarding these transactions. However, no legal action was initiated, and, in fact, by the time of the ICC report, the Harriman syndicate no longer controlled the Chicago & Alton. As we will see later, the ICC investigation was an act of vindictiveness ordered by President Theodore Roosevelt or his close aides following Roosevelt's break with Harriman over campaign financing in 1906.

Following the ICC investigation, a sharp debate regarding Harriman's actions and the Chicago & Alton developed between Professor William Z. Ripley of Harvard University and Harriman's biographer, George Kennan. In this controversy Professor Ripley supported the ICC's criticism while Mr. Kennan defended Harriman.

Ripley put the case against Harriman in strong terms:

Practically all of the possible abuses or frauds described in the preceding pages under the caption of stock-watering are found combined in a single instance in recent years—the reorganization of the Chicago & Alton by the late E. H. Harriman and his associates during the eight years following 1898. The case is an illuminating one; for it shows how an unscrupulous management may, at one and the same time, enormously enrich insiders at the expense of the investing public, and prejudice the interests of shippers, both by crippling the road physically and by creating the need for high rates for service in order to support the fraudulent capitalization.[1]

Ripley's basic case is that prior to 1898, "the Alton roads had been conservatively financed, in the face of a profitable and constantly expanding business," but that the Harriman syndicate's operations left it in financial shambles with considerable "water" in the road's net capitalization and the road's average net capitalization ($66,000 per mile owned) above that of all U. S. railroads. Ripley did concede that the refinancing substituted bonds and guaranteed stock with lower rates of interest for bonds and common stock that formerly received higher rates of interest and dividends so that interest requirements did not expand in proportion to indebtedness.

The problem as seen by Ripley was twofold. First was the burden of the new indebtedness when it matured. Second, real ownership and control of the property were split because the real value was represented by the bonds outstanding while management of the road was in the hands of the owners of the stock which was worthless. Both of these statements are either wrong or subject to considerable qualification.

Kennan's defense of Harriman seeks first to establish that while the Chicago & Alton Railroad was profitable in the 1890s, it was also very conservatively managed and in a poor state of repair due to the neglect of the management. The Alton's record of high dividends was to some extent purchased at the cost of inadequate improvement, repair, and equipment expenditures. Kennan engages in a lengthy point-by-point rebuttal of Ripley's charges. One point worth noting is that the Chicago & Alton's business rather than "constantly expanding," as stated by Ripley, was declining in the 1890s. Gross earnings of the Alton were $8.9 million in 1887, but only $6.3 million in 1898. This is one of several points that Ripley clearly misstated in his zeal to condemn the financial transactions of the Harriman syndicate. Kennan concludes that the Harriman syndicate's financial transactions were legal (as did the ICC in its report), above board, and that they left the Alton a better road physically in 1907 than when they took it over in 1899. The latter conclusion is supported by more dispassionate observers.

In evaluating Kennan's position on the Chicago & Alton reorganization it should be noted that before he thoroughly investigated the reorganization he agreed with Ripley's position. In a letter to Norman Firth (27 August 1923) Kennan wrote:

When I began my study of Mr. Harriman's life I had a very strong bias against him and I did not decide to undertake the work until I investigated thoroughly the Chicago & Alton reorganization on which my adverse bias was largely based. If I had found anything "crooked" or indefensible in that, I should have declined to write the biography because I am not in the whitewashing business. In this case, however, as in my investigation of the Siberian exile system, I found that the bias with which I started was all wrong and wholly unjustifiable.[2]

Kennan did not believe that the Harriman syndicate profited unduly from its transactions with the Chicago & Alton. HIs evidence for this conclusion, in addition to disputing the profit estimates for the syndicate by the ICC and others, is a statement by an eminent English authority on American railroads, Robert Fleming, who was also an investor in the Harriman syndicate. According to Fleming, the whole profit of the Alton syndicate "was only eight percent—about five percent per annum—nothing very extraordinary surely."[3]

On the crucial question of the weight of fixed charges, Kennan argues that the capitalization of the Chicago & Alton was prudent and conservative. He bases this on a comparison of net traffic earnings ($4,415,974) in the last year of Harriman control (1907) and of the interest and dividend payments of $3,533,440 on capitalization of $101,086,000. This comparison suggests a reasonable margin of safety; it suffers, however, from three errors. First, average net earnings for 1899–1907 were $3.52 million. The 1907 figure is the highest for the period. Second, the fixed cost figure is incorrect because it includes a 4 percent dividend on $39,086,000 of stock ($563,440), but does not include amortization and interest payments then (1907) required on equipment obligation notes ($786,617), nor interest on $6 million in 5 percent collateral trust notes ($300,000) and $174,000 in Mississippi River Bridge bonds ($10,440), and $35,172 in required dividends on prior lien and participating stock. In addition, the interest on the 3 percent Chicago & Alton bonds is shown for $40 million of such bonds. This is too high.

While the total of the bonds outstanding was $45,350,000, interest was paid on only $37,530,000 because $8 million was deposited as security against the collateral trust notes. The correct fixed charge, as we shall see below, is almost the same total ($3,263,753), but its composition is rather different. Finally, Kennan does not satisfactorily answer Ripley's main point—the burden of debt repayment. For the Chicago & Alton fifty-year bonds, an annual sinking fund payment of $322,427 would be required with a 5 percent return and $441,156 with a 4 percent return. No sinking fund was established by the Harriman syndicate. However, the point Kennan should have made in this regard is that a sinking fund is not necessarily required for prudent management and at the time was not customary in railroad management. Based on the experience of several decades of falling interest rates, it was generally expected that the mortgage could be refinanced with a lower interest rate bond when it came due. It would be difficult, perhaps impossible, to find a railroad in the United States at this time that made sinking fund contributions sufficient to pay off its debt when due. The physical assets of railroads were viewed as being of enduring value unlike the physical assets of industrial concerns.

Reorganization of the Chicago & Alton

We see a sharp difference of opinion in the literature regarding the Harriman management of the Chicago & Alton. A review of the accepted facts of the case will be helpful to establish a basis for evaluation of the Harriman management of the Chicago & Alton and the debate on that management.

In the 1890s the Chicago & Alton was indeed a poorly managed railroad. Its gross earnings had declined from $8.9 million in 1887 to $6.3 million in 1898. Dividends had averaged around 8 percent per year in the mid-1890s, but by 1898 were down to 7 percent. The Alton had not provided adequate allowance for maintenance and depreciation. A sinking fund was maintained but the annual contribution varied widely (from $9,030 to $169,986), the average for the seven years 1892–1898 was $82,225. In 1898 the railroad showed an income balance surplus of $3,005,576 and cash and other assets of $1,175,945. Dividend payments averaged $1,648,101 for the period 1892–1898 with $1,556,142 paid in 1898. From these figures it seems clear that the road could stand some improvement in management, but also that it had considerable attractiveness for take-over by outsiders.

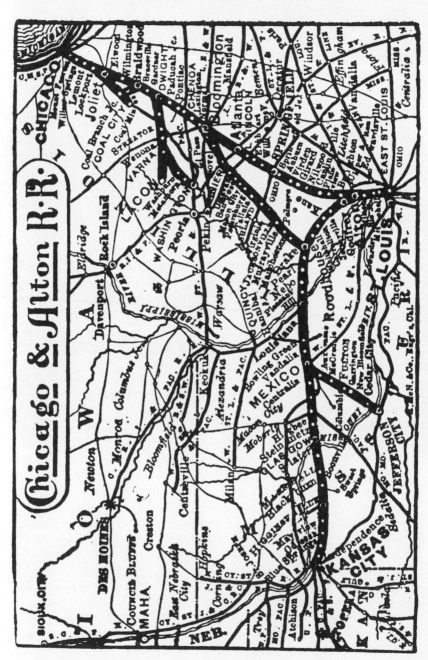

4. The Chicago and Alton Railroad

The main managerial weakness of T. B. Blackstone, the Chicago & Alton's president, was his failure to merge with a larger railroad earlier. Merger with the Santa Fe before its Kansas City-Chicago line was built in the 1880s was a possibility Blackstone rejected. Such weakness in management of a smaller firm is not unusual. The incentive to protect the job security of the incumbent management is strong and that often works to the disadvantage of equity owners in the firm. The Chicago & Alton under Blackstone in the 1890s is a classic example. Rather than robbing them, as Ripley mistakenly charges, Harriman in effect rescued the stockholders of the Chicago & Alton in his reorganization.

The organizers of the Harriman syndicate in 1899 were E. H. Harriman, Jacob H. Schiff, James Stillman, and George Gould. Harriman undertook the reorganization of the Chicago & Alton after being asked by some major stockholders (some of whom became members of his syndicate) to take the road over from Blackstone. An investigation of the railroad and a favorable report on its possibilities by S. M. Felton encouraged Harriman to proceed.

The Harriman syndicate included about 100 members. Harriman and his associates gained control of the Chicago & Alton by the purchase of almost all the firm's common and preferred stock for 175 and 200 respectively. The announced policy of the syndicate was to put the railroad in first-class condition and to develop it as a link in the larger Harriman system. These policies were carried out with the refinancing and very substantial increase in capitalization that is the basis for the controversy over the Harriman management of the Chicago & Alton.

The first step in refinancing the Chicago & Alton was the sale of $32 million of 3 percent refunding mortgage bonds of the railroad to the syndicate members at 65. The members apparently profited from the later resale of these bonds. The ICC estimated that the average resale was 90 which would give $8 million profit to the syndicate members. This would mean the resale implied a yield of 3.3 percent versus the 4.6 percent yield of the sale at 65.

The bond issue just discussed provided the cash for the syndicate's second step, which was a special 30 percent dividend of $6,669,000. The two transactions created an increase in liabilities of $32 million but left only $13,410,000 for refunding and improvements. In terms of the books, this was resolved by writing up assets by $12,444,177.66 with a corresponding credit to "construction expenditures uncapitalized." The bond discount and special dividend were charged against the latter account and the debit balance ($996,600, 30 June 1900) was transferred to profit and loss. This was justified by the argument that past reinvestment of earnings had been charged to expenses rather than being capitalized. Following this line of argument, the bonds in excess of additions to property were simply a capitalization of this past investment.

In 1900 the Chicago & Alton Railway Company was formed as a holding company to take over the stock of the operating railroad. The holding company sold its stockholders $22 million of 3-1/2 percent collateral trust bonds at 60. Notice the implied yield of 5.8 percent. The proceeds were used to purchase the older preferred stock ($3,472,200 face value for which the syndicate had paid $6,944,440) for $10 million and the St. Louis, Peoria & Northern Railway from the Harriman syndicate for $3 million. This second issue of bonds provided another potential source of profit to the syndicate because the market price ranged from 78 to 86-1/2 (providing comfortable yields of 4.5 to 4 percent) over the next two to three years. In exchange for $18,322,400 of the old common stock of the Chicago & Alton Railroad, the holding company issued $19,489,000 of its own preferred and $19,542,800 of common stock.

The last transaction by the syndicate was consolidation of the holding and operating companies in 1906. The only increase in capitalization with the consolidation was the issuance of $879,300 in "prior lien and participating" stock to take up the small outside holdings of the original railroad stocks.

Table 7–1 presents an estimate of the cost of the Chicago & Alton Railroad, as it stood on 31 June 1900, to the Harriman syndicate. The original purchase of control cost the syndicate $39 million. The bond transactions and extra cash dividend reduced the cost to $10.4 million. Purchase of the St. Louis, Peoria & Northern Railway added $3 million for a total cost of $13.4 million. This includes an estimate of almost $12 million in profits from the bond transactions. This estimate is undoubtedly an overstatement.

The controlling interest in the Chicago & Alton Railroad shifted in the following years. In 1904 the company came under the joint control of the Union Pacific and the Rock Island Railroads. The Union Pacific (controlled by Harriman) purchased a majority of the preferred stock and the Rock Island bought some of the preferred stock and nearly all the common. The Rock Island's sale of its stock to the Toledo, St. Louis & Western Railway in August 1907 transferred control of the Chicago & Alton to the Toledo, St. Louis & Western Railway and out of the hands of the Harriman syndicate. The latter railroad acquired the stock, giving it control of the Chicago & Alton in exchange for a new issue of collat-

Table 7–1
Cost of Chicago & Alton Railroad
to Harriman Syndicate

Cost:				
Common Stock	$18,322,400	175	=	$32,064,200
Preferred Stock	$ 3,476,200	200	=	6,944,400
				$39,008,600

Less:		
Profit from bond transactions (1899)[a]	=	8,000,000
Extra Cash dividend	=	6,669,000
Purchase by Chicago & Alton Railway (1900) of		
$3,472,200 of old preferred	=	10,000,000
Profit from bond transactions (1900)[b]	=	3,960,000
		$10,379,600

Plus:		
Purchase of St. Louis, Peoria & Northern Railway	=	3,000,000
NET COST		$13,379,000

[a]ICC estimate.
[b]Purchased at 60 and resold at 78.

eral trust bonds. The Union Pacific retained about $10 million in preferred stock but lost control of the Chicago & Alton. About ten years later the Union Pacific interests again assumed direction when both the Chicago & Alton and the Toledo, St. Louis & Western got into financial difficulties.

There is some debate about the Harriman syndicate's control after 1904. Table 7–2 shows the board of directors from 1900 through October 1907. It is clear that Harriman supporters had a majority on the board (6 of 11) through the 1906 elections, probably in October. Moreover, until that election Harriman was the chairman of the executive committee. This fits with the agreement between the Chicago & Alton and the Rock Island whereby a controlling number of shares were deposited by them with the Central Trust Company of New York to be held in a voting trust. Under this agreement, control was to alternate yearly between the rivals (6 of 11 board members) starting after October 1906. Despite appearances, the board, as of 1 June 1907, was probably not a Harriman board because the chairman of the executive committee was a Chicago &

Table 7–2
Board of Directors
Chicago & Alton Railroad (1901)
and
Chicago & Alton Railway (1902–1907)

Elected 2 April 1900

E.H. Harriman	R.C. Clowry	J.C. Hutchins
C.H. Chappell	S.M. Felton	W.H. Henkie
M.L. Schiff	W.A. Simonson	
	S.M. Felton, President	

Elected 2 October 1901 (Also 2 October 1902 and 6 October 1903)

C.H. Chappell	James B. Forgan	E.H. Harriman
F.S. Winston	David R. Francis	John J. Mitchell
S.M. Felton	George J. Gould	Norman B. Ream
M.L. Schiff	James Stillman	
	S.M. Felton, President	

Elected 4 October 1904

Term expires in 1905	Term expires in 1906	Term expires in 1907
W.H. Moore	W.B. Leeds	J.H. Moore
E.H. Harriman*	S.M. Felton*	D.G. Reid
Norman B. Ream*	John J. Mitchell*	Robert Mather
James B. Forgan*	James Stillman*	
E.H. Harriman, Chairman, Executive Committee		
S.M. Felton, President		

Rock Island man. While S. M. Felton (a long-time Harriman man) was newly reelected to the board, he was also still president of the Chicago & Rock Island and probably then owed allegiance to the latter rather than to Harriman. Thus, the apparent Harriman majority as of 1 June 1907 is misleading.

For our own purposes, Harriman syndicate control of the Chicago & Alton will be analyzed for the period including fiscal years 1900 through 1907. The syndicate certainly had control through October 1906. The Rock Island took control sometime during fiscal 1907. Fiscal year 1908 was to see Harriman control. Instead the Toledo, St. Louis & Western purchased control in August 1907 and was firmly in control, as shown by the board elected on 2 October 1907.

Table 7–2 (cont'd)

As of 1 June 1906		
Term expires in 1906	Term expires in 1907	Term expires in 1908
S.M. Felton*	E.H. Harriman*	James B. Forgan*
John J. Mitchell*	Robert Mather	B.F. Yoakum
W.F. Moore	James Stillman*	James H. Moore
D.G. Reid		Norman Ream*

E.H. Harriman, Chairman, Executive Committee
S.M. Felton, President

As 1 June 1907		
Term expires in 1907	Term expires in 1908	Term expires in 1909
E.H. Harriman*	James B. Forgan*	S.M. Felton*
Robert Mather	B.F. Yoakum	John J. Mitchell*
James Stillman*	James H. Moore	W.H. Moore
	Norman B. Ream*	O.G. Reid

B.F. Yoakum, Chairman, Executive Committee
S.M. Felton, President

Elected 2 october 1907		
Term expires in 1908	Term expires in 1909	Term expires in 1909
Geo. H. Ross	S.M. Felton*	Edwin Hawley
Norman B. Ream*	John J. Mitchell*	Thos. H. Hubbard
F.H. Davis	T.P. Shonts	Henry E. Huntington
	Wm. G. Beale	

Thos. H. Hubbard, Chairman, Executive Committee
T.P. Shonts, President

*Members of original Chicago & Alton Railway Board who continued as board members after 4 October 1904.

Profitability of the Chicago & Alton

Earlier investigators did not examine the profitability of the Chicago & Alton under Harriman management as a means of evaluating that management's performance. Table 7–3 presents estimates of the real (1900$) economic (internal) rate of return for the Chicago & Alton Railroad's operations for alternate time periods and investment cost basis. For the Chicago & Alton Railroad on the basis of book cost through 1891 and investment expenditure for 1892–1899, the internal rate of return with the Harriman syndicate's actual cost is a very substantial 15.3 percent—

Table 7–3
Estimated Internal Rates of Return
(percent)

Period	Chicago & Alton Railroad[a]
1892–1899	4.8
1900–1907 (Actual)	15.3
1900–1907 (Hypothetical)[b]	3.6
1908–1918	6.4

[a]Investment cost is book cost through 1899 plus investment cost for 1899–1907 (and 1908–1918).

[b]Actual cost is that of Table 7–1 plus investment cost for 1899–1907. Hypothetical cost is cost of purchase of control of the Chicago & Alton Railroad plus investment cost for 1899–1907. It is assumed that only enough new bonds are issued to refund old debt and pay for investment expenditure. In this hypothetical, there is no extra 30 percent dividend, nor any profits made by the syndicate from bond sales.

over three times the rate of return in the preceding period. The Harriman management and financial transactions significantly raised the operating profitability of the railroad. Note that this result depends to an important extent on the substantial reduction of their investment cost which the syndicate achieved through its financial transactions. If we take the hypothetical cost rate of return for 1900–1907 in Table 7–3 (discussed in detail below), the estimated interal rate of return on the road's operations is only 3.6 percent, three-fourths of the rate for the preceding period. Thus, the Harriman refinancing was essential both for improvment of the Chicago & Alton and for its profitability in the Harriman period. Harriman's master stroke was heavy concentration on bond financing when interest rates were at their historic low. In the immediate pre-Harriman period the Chicago & Alton was marginally unprofitable and it would have been definitely unprofitable during the Harriman period without the refinancing. Without the refinancing the Chicago & Alton was worth about one-third what the Harriman syndicate paid for it. Thus, the old owners of the road also gained substantially from the refinancing. The rate of return during the period of the Toledo, St. Louis & Western's control (1908–1918) was a little less than half that of the Harriman period. In the latter period the Chicago & Alton was at best marginally profitable.

Table 7–4 presents the annual gross accounting rates of return for the

Chicago & Alton. Gross capital for 1892 to 1898 is the 1892 book value of road and equipment plus annual investment. For 1899 to 1907 gross capital is the syndicate cost of purchase of the Chicago & Alton plus the cumulative reported expenditures on additions, improvements, and equipment. During 1908–1918 gross capital is 1907 gross capital plus investment expenditure in 1908–1918.

The financing activities of the Harriman syndicate described earlier make book value of road and equipment a considerable overstatement of the value of physical capital for 1899–1907. For example, in 1907 the book value of franchises and property is $107.5 million. This plus additions, improvements, and equipment in the preceding fifteen months

Table 7–4
Gross Accounting Rate of Return
Chicago & Alton Railroad[a]

Year[b]	Gross Capital (000 1900$)	Capital Earnings (000 1900$)	Gross Accounting Rate of Return (%)
1892	$34,924	$2,418	6.9
1893	34,924	2,371	6.8
1894	37,237	2,378	6.4
1895	37,237	2,799	7.5
1896	37,237	2,860	7.7
1897	37,237	2,504	6.7
1898	37,237	1,964	5.3
1899	39,321	2,435	6.5
		Mean rate of return	6.7
1900	15,372	2,836	18.4
1901	19,601	2,914	14.9
1902	19,911	2,492	12.5
1903	20,492	2,687	13.1
1904	22,042	3,113	14.1
1905	25,612	3,363	13.1
1906	26,579	2,878	10.8
1907	30,119	3,593	11.9
		Mean rate of return	13.7

[a]Data are from the company reports in Poor, *Manual of Railroads*, annual volumes 1900–1909.

[b]Year ending 31 December for 1892–1899, and ending 30 June for 1900–1907.

($4.1 million) would give a book value of $111.6 million, which is more than triple the 1907 estimate of gross physical capital used here.

The mean rate of return for the 1892–1899 period (6.7 percent) is about half that of the Harriman period (13.7 percent). Thus, in terms of the gross profitability ratio as well as the economic (internal) rate of return, the Chicago & Alton was quite profitable and on the average for 1900–1907 more than twice as profitable as in the preceding period. Notice that this (as well as the economic rate of return) is markedly higher than the 8 percent rate of return suggested by Robert Fleming above. However, the mean estimate here (13.7 percent) is within the range cited by Kennan when he wrote that the prices at which the syndicate sold their securities would give them "a profit of probably eight percent and possibly twelve or fifteen percent upon their total cash investment."[4]

Despite a 50 percent increase in operating expenses per mile for 1900–1907 compared to 1892–1899, and $11 million more investment for the Chicago & Alton with Harriman's financing, the railroad was far more profitable in the later period than in the earlier. Moreover, this appears to be almost entirely the result of Harriman's management and financing, the much maligned financing playing the crucial role.

The gross profit ratios for the Chicago & Alton under Toledo, St. Louis & Western control (1908–1918) are shown in Table 7–5. The average ratio (14.2 percent) for the first three years (1908–1910) is higher than that for the Harriman period. This is not a product of the Reid-Moore management but is a continuation of the impetus and improvements of the Harriman management. The Reid-Moore management did not have Harriman's vision in either finance or railroad improvement. As the new management's deeds are increasingly reflected in the bottom line, the rate of return declines precipitously with the 1911–1918 mean being only 5.0 percent (about one-third that of the earlier periods). It seems clear that this change is a product of (among other things) the new management, not the Harriman syndicate's actions. The decline in earnings was general in the industry at this time and was in part the result of the ICC freezing rates while costs rose sharply.

Physical Condition of the Chicago & Alton

Professor Ripley charged that the Harriman syndicate "crippled" the Chicago & Alton "physically." This is a rather strange charge and must rank with the statement that the Chicago & Alton of the 1890s was doing "constantly expanding business' as an error or misstatement by Ripley.

Table 7-5
Gross Profit Ratios
Chicago & Alton Railroad
under Control of Toledo, St. Louis & Western Railroad
Company

Year[b]	Gross Capital[a] (000 1900$)	Gross Capital Earnings (000 1900$)	Gross Profit Ratio (%)
1908	$23,493	$3,505	14.9
1909	24,592	3,876	15.8
1910	25,968	3,052	11.8
1911	27,640	2,624	9.5
1912	28,000	2,169	7.7
1913	28,543	1,041	3.6
1914	29,224	612	2.1
1915	30,975	980	3.2
1916	31,040	1,816	5.9
1917	31,256	1,447	4.6
1918	31,739	1,037	3.3
		Mean rate of return	7.5

[a]1898 book value plus cumulative investment (additions, improvements, and betterments) for 1899–1918.

[b]Year ending 30 June. The year of 1916 is reported for both 30 June and 31 December with 1917 and 1918 figures for capital stock and gross capital earnings estimated for year ending 30 June.

No one can deny that the Harriman management immensely improved the physical condition of the Chicago & Alton. Apparently there was still considerable deferred maintenance to be done when Harriman lost control in 1907, but the road he left was physically far superior to the one he took over in 1899.

Table 7–6 provides a view of the physical productivity of the Chicago & Alton over the period 1892–1907. Both passenger and freight productivity as measured by passenger miles per mile and freight ton miles per mile of operated road are significantly higher during the Harriman administration than in the preceding Blackstone administration and increase substantially in the former while they are flat or decline in the latter. It should be noted that five years of the 1892–1899 period were depression years. This in part accounts for the flatness or decline of passenger and freight productivity for the Chicago & Alton in the 1890s. Passenger

Table 7–6
Chicago & Alton Railroad[a]
Passenger and Freight Output Per Mile of Road

Year	Miles of Railroad Operated	Passenger Miles Per Mile (000)	Freight Ton Miles Per Mile (000)
1892	842.36	156.7	659.1
1893	842.21	187.6	573.7
1894	842.21	117.1	502.4
1895	842.21	131.1	587.6
1896	842.21	124.2	630.5
1897	843.54	121.2	669.8
1898	843.54	124.3	588.2
1899	843.54	137.2	660.9
Mean	842.73	137.4	609.0
1900	919.64	130.9	685.0
1901	919.64	144.5	895.0
1902	919.64	150.7	981.6
1903	915.41	160.4	1,204.7
1904	917.31	187.3	1,196.5
1905	915.23	231.6	1,103.1
1906	970.33	171.1	1,210.6
1907	970.33	186.3	1,429.4
Mean	931.19	170.4	1,088.2

[a]Data from Poor, *Manual of Railroads,* annual volumes 1900–1909.

miles per mile are 42 percent higher in 1907 than in 1900, while freight ton miles per mile are 109 percent higher in 1907 than 1900. This compares with the general downward trend in passenger miles per mile and a slight downward (or flat) trend in freight tons per mile during 1892–1899.

For all U. S. roads, freight ton miles per mile of road between 1900 and 1907 grew 32 percent compared to 109 percent for the Chicago & Alton. Passenger miles per mile of road for all U. S. roads grew 36 percent from 1900 to 1907, almost as rapidly as the Chicago & Alton. Overall, the Chicago & Alton significantly outpaced the U. S. average during the period of Harriman control. This clearly illustrates that more is at work here than simply the comparison of a prosperous period with a depression period.

The growth of the coal trade was apparently an important factor in the expansion of freight movement on the Chicago & Alton during the Harriman administration. Blackstone had actually viewed the earlier proportional decline of the coal trade as a good thing. Connection with the larger Harriman system and the addition of two branch roads (the St. Louis, Peoria & Northern Railway from Springfield to Grove, Illinois, 57.56 miles; and the Quincy, Carrelton & St. Louis Railway from Eldred to Litchfield, Illinois, 48.8 miles) are undoubtedly also factors. The physical productivity illustrated in Table 7–6 strongly suggests improvement of the road rather than "physical crippling."

The Harriman physical and management improvement of the Chicago & Alton is reflected in the movement of the railroad's average passenger and freight rates over the 1899–1907 period. These rates are shown in Table 7–7. In terms of 1900 dollars, the passenger rate declines to 84

Table 7–7
Chicago & Alton
Average Passenger and Freight Rates[a]

Year	Average Passenger Rates[b] per mile		Average Freight Rates[c] per ton mile	
	actual	1900 = 100[d]	actual	1900 = 100[d]
	(cents)		(cents)	
1899	1.92	2.07	0.80	0.86
1900	1.90	1.90	0.79	0.79
1901	1.94	1.97	0.72	0.73
1902	1.86	1.77	0.68	0.65
1903	1.98	1.87	0.60	0.57
1904	1.95	1.84	0.68	0.64
1905	1.73	1.62	0.69	0.65
1906	2.05	1.86	0.64	0.58
1907	2.02	1.74	0.60	0.52

[a]Source: Annual volumes of Poor, *Manual of Railroads.*
[b]Revenue per passenger mile.
[c]Revenue per freight ton mile.
[d]Based on Bureau of Labor Statistics Wholesale Price Index from *Historical Statistics of the United States* with 1900 set equal to 100.

percent of its 1899 level by 1907 while the freight rate falls to 60 percent of its 1899 level. This compares with 81 percent for the passenger mile rate for all U. S. roads over the same period and 83 percent for the freight ton mile rate for all U. S. roads. Consumers of railroad services gained significantly from the Harriman improvement and refinancing of the Chicago & Alton.

Chicago & Alton Financial Condition

The final element necessary to evaluate the Harriman management of the Chicago & Alton is an examination of the change in the road's financial condition between 1899 and 1907. Table 7–8 presents an overview of the fixed payments of the Chicago & Alton in 1899, while Table 7–9 shows the same information for 1907.

In 1899 the Chicago & Alton appeared to be in excellent financial condition. Its fixed payments of $770,777 left $1,913,914 out of the net traffic earnings for dividends, sinking funds, etc. The railroad did have about $8.2 million in bonds due within the next four years. There seems little doubt that these could be refinanced and probably at a much lower rate of interest than the 6 and 7 percent they were paying in 1899. Against this must be set the fact that gross revenue, net traffic earnings, and the rate of return on operations had all been falling in the 1890s. Clearly the road needed rejuvenation and substantial investment.

Between 1899 and 1907 investment in additions, improvements, and equipment totalled $20,752,800. If this plus the bonds due in 1900 and 1903 had been refinanced at 3 percent and, assuming the necessary bonds were sold at 80, fixed interest charges would have been $1,158,000. This is the hypothetical financing case described above. With the 1899 guaranteed dividends, total fixed charges would have been $1,410,000. Even with 1899 net traffic earnings this would have left $1,275,000 for sinking funds and dividends after fixed payments and lease rentals. For the amount of bonds involved, a fifty-year sinking fund at a conservative 3 percent would require $334,092, leaving $940,908 for dividends. With 1907 net traffic earnings ($4,415,974) the financing described would leave $2,430,858 for dividends after fixed payments, lease rentals, and sinking fund. The 1907 potential for dividends, etc., would have been 2.6 times that of 1899 with the hypothetical financing.

The actual 1907 financial situation after the Harriman syndicate's financial transactions is rather different from the hypothetical situation discussed above, as shown in Table 7–8. Fixed payments in 1907 totaled

Table 7–8
Fixed Payments
Chicago & Alton Railroad[a]
(1899)

Due Date	Funded Debt: Item	Balance	Interest Rate (%)	Interest Due
1 May 1903	Sinking Fund Chicago & Alton RR.	$1,663,000	6	$ 99,780
1 July 1903	Consolidated Chicago & Alton RR.	4,379,850	6	262,791
1 Aug. 1900	Louisiana & Missouri River RR. First mtge.	1,785,000	7	124,950
1 Nov. 1900	Louisiana & Missouri River RR. Second mtge.	300,000	7	21,000
1 Oct. 1912	Missouri River Bridge 1st mtge.	170,000	6	10,000
			TOTAL	$518,721
	Guaranteed Dividends:			
	Joliet and Chicago RR.	$1,500,000	7	$105,000
	Louisiana & Missouri River RR. (preferred)	329,000	7	23,030
	Kansas City, St. Louis & Chicago RR. (preferred)	1,750,000	6	105,000
	Kansas City, St. Louis & Chicago RR. (common)	271,800	7	19,026
			TOTAL	$252,056
			GRAND TOTAL	$770,777

[a]Data from Poor, *Manual of Railroads,* 1900, pp. 656–57.

$3,263,753. Even with the 1907 net traffic earnings this leaves only $1,152,221 for sinking funds, dividends, etc. For the Chicago & Alton fifty-year bonds, an annual sinking fund contribution of $332,427 would be required with a 5 percent return, $441,156 with a 4 percent return, and $597,091 with a 3 percent return. With a 5 percent sinking fund only $819,794 would be left for dividends, 87 percent of 1899. Notice, however, that the stock owners (the Harriman syndicate) made their profit

Table 7–9
Fixed Payments
Chicago & Alton Railroad[a]
(1907)

Due Date	Funded Debt: Item	Balance	Interest Rate	Interest Due
1 Oct. 1949	Chicago & Alton RR. refunding mortgage	$45,350,000[b]	3	$1,120,500
1 July 1950	Chicago & Alton Ry. first lien	22,000,000	3.5	770,000
1 Jan. 1912	Chicago & Alton Ry. Collateral trust rates	6,000,000	5	300,000
1 Oct. 1912	Mississippi River Bridge first mortgage	174,000	6	10,440
			TOTAL	$2,220,940
	Equipment Obligations:			
15 Dec. 1912	Joint notes, Chicago & Alton RR. and Mobile & Ohio	104,500	4	4,180
15 May 1912	Chicago & Alton RR. Series A notes	195,000	5	9,750
1 Sept. 1913	Chicago & Alton RR. Series B notes	611,000	5	30,550
1 Sept. 1913	Chicago & Alton RR. Series C notes	1,666,000	4	66,640
1 Nov. 1915	Chicago & Alton RR. Series D notes	2,034,000	4	81,360
1 June 1916	Notes to Pullman Company	76,064	5	3,803
			TOTAL	$196,283
	Principal payments on equipment obligations			590,334
	Prior lien and participating stock			35,172
	Guaranteed dividends (leases)			241,024
			GRAND TOTAL	$3,263,753

[a]Data from Poor, *Manual of Railroads*, 1908, pp. 364–65.

[b]$8 million on deposit as security against the $6 million in collateral trust notes. Poor, *Manual of Railroads*, 1908, p. 365.

from the financial transactions and did not need to depend on dividends. Ripley and the ICC charged that the Harriman financing made the Chicago & Alton stocks worthless. We see that its action did reduce their value, but it is incorrect that they were made worthless. In 1909 the average New York Stock Exchange bid for Chicago & Alton common varied from 57-7/8 to 74-3/4 and preferred from 70 to 78-1/2. On 31 December 1909 common was 66-1/4 and preferred 70 compared to 68 and 77 respectively a year earlier. While this is significantly less than the Harriman syndicate paid for stock, it is not worthless. Thus, Ripley's second main point about the division between real value of the railroad and its management is incorrect.

One should treat the hypothetical financing described with a great deal of caution. It is not certain that such financing was in fact possible. In particular it needs to be observed that while the bonds sold to the syndicate were resold at higher prices, this occurred over a period of two to three years. Sale of the bonds to the syndicate raised the funds immediately. Improvement of the railroad could then proceed at once. The higher prices of the bonds in the next two or three years then reflected in part the physical and management improvements already in place. The later rise in the bond prices was made possible by the earlier sale of the bonds to the syndicate.

Summary

From the analysis that we have seen here it can be concluded that the Harriman management and financing markedly improved the profitability of the operation of the Chicago & Alton Railroad. The physical productivity figures also indicate a very significant improvement during the Harriman period. This plus the general consensus of physical improvement of the road indicates the incorrectness of Ripley's charge that the Harriman syndicate crippled the road physically. Thus, in terms of profitability during its tenure, physical productivity of the road, and the physical condition of the road, the Harriman syndicate did an excellent job, showing the usual hallmarks of Harriman's skill and genius. Ripley's bile toward Harriman originates not from fact, but from value judgments and simple wrongheadedness.

In the matter of the road's financial condition the situation is complex and easily misunderstood. Capitalized at 5 percent, the implicit 2.1 percent dividend in 1907 with a 5 percent sinking fund would yield a share

Table 7–10
Fixed Payments
Chicago & Alton Railroad[a]
(1918)

Due Date	Funded Debt: Item	Balance	Interest Rate	Interest Due
1 Oct. 1949	Chicago & Alton RR. Refunding Mortgage	$45,350,000	3	$1,300,500
1 July 1950	Chicago & Alton Ry. First Lien	22,000,000	3.5	770,000
1 June 1922	Chicago & Alton RR. Sinking Fund	750,000	5	37,500
1 March 1930	Chicago & Alton RR. Improvement & Equipment	6,817,000	5	[b]
1 July 1932	Chicago & Alton RR. General Gold 6's	16,834,000	6	1,010,040
			TOTAL	$3,118,040
	Equipment Trust Notes:			
1 Feb. 1919	Series F	$ 12,000	4.5	$ 540
1 Oct. 1920	Series G	146,000	5	7,300
1 Dec. 1921	Series "1916"	285,000	4.5	12,865
			TOTAL	$ 20,665
	Principal payments on equipment trust notes			$ 180,000
	Guaranteed dividends (leases)			233,030
	Prior lien and participating stock			35,172
			TOTAL	$ 448,202
			GRAND TOTAL	$3,586,907

[a]Data from Poor, *Manual of Railroads,* 1919, pp. 1531–32.
[b]All pledged as collateral for GeneralGold 6/s.

value of 42 compared to 175 for common and 200 for preferred when the Harriman syndicate bought the stock in 1899. In terms of the ratio of par value of exchanged securities, the Toledo, St. Louis & Western Railway paid 49 for the stock, giving it control in 1907. In fact, repayment of the equipment obligations over the next few years would have added $786,617 to monies available for dividends, etc., if earnings stayed at the 1907 level. With a 5 percent sinking fund this would have allowed a 4.1 percent dividend on all stock. Capitalized at 5 percent, the stock would have been worth 82 compared with the implicit 49 paid by the

Toledo, St. Louis & Western Railway. Unfortunately, earnings did not remain at the 1907 level and this happy outcome did not materialize. The syndicate could be faulted for committing the road to fixed payments that allowed little cushion for the inevitable bad year(s). While with the clarity of hindsight this might be considered a failure of prudent (in this case ultraconservative) management, it certainly was not "looting" as charged by Ripley. Rather than sitting in their rocking chairs collecting dividends over a long period of time, the Harriman syndicate used some ingenious financing to collect their Chicago & Alton profit. Contrary to the Ripley and ICC allegations, the investing public did not lose as a result of this financing.

As a final word, it should be noted that any financial difficulties of the Chicago & Alton after 1907 were severely exacerbated by the Toledo, St. Louis & Western management and the action of the ICC in freezing rates while costs climbed sharply. Table 7–10 (compare with Table 7–8) shows Chicago & Alton Railroad fixed payments in fiscal 1918. The total is 10 percent higher than in fiscal 1907. Worse yet, the total on bonds is 42 percent higher. Bonded indebtedness in 1907 was almost $74 million. In 1918 it had been increased to almost $92 million, a rise of 25 percent. The Harriman syndicate financing did increase the riskiness of the financial situation for the Chicago & Alton; however, it was the management and financial operations of the Toledo, St. Louis & Western that made a potentially bad situation bad with certainty. The ultimate blame for the Chicago & Alton's later financial condition rests with the latter (and the ICC), not with the Harriman syndicate.

CHAPTER EIGHT

Minor Plays: The Kansas City Southern, the Baltimore & Ohio, and the Erie Railroad Company

The Kansas City Southern

During the prime of his career (1898–1909) Harriman was involved in a relatively minor way with several railroads in addition to the major ones we have already considered. This chapter examines his activities with the most important of these minor involvements: the Kansas City Southern, the Balitmore & Ohio, and the Erie Railroad Company, starting with the Kansas City Southern.

A group of western entrepreneurs in 1889 received a charter for a railroad from Kansas City to Fort Smith, Arkansas. The projected road ran through the small town of Nevada, Missouri, and was incorporated as the Kansas City, Nevada & Fort Scott Railway. On 1 October 1892 the first eighty-one miles of the road were completed and put into operation. No further extension of the line was accomplished until after reorganization of the railroad on 26 January 1893. The new owners had a broader vision of where they were bound and renamed the road the Kansas City, Pittsburgh & Gulf. The Pittsburgh in this name was a growing town in the Kansas coal region. By 30 June 1894 a total of 207 miles were in operation.

The new group of promoters was headed by Arthur E. Stilwell of Kansas City, a successful insurance and real estate entrepreneur. Stilwell was initially the first vice-president, but by 1896 had been elevated to president. The principal goal of the projected railroad was to capture a significant portion of the export traffic of the Missouri River region. In the early nineties that traffic was largely carried by the Illinois Central, especially the portion going south to the Gulf of Mexico. Stilwell and his associates organized several construction companies to build the proposed railroad. The Panic of 1893 and the following long period of business depression both increased the difficulty of raising the necessary capital and reduced the potential business of the fledgling railroad. Because of these factors the road was not completed and put into operation as a whole until 1898. It then ran from Kansas City to Port Arthur on the Gulf of Mexico, with a total length of 778 miles.

As a real estate operator rather than an experienced railroad builder and manager, Stilwell (with his associates) appears to have stressed the real estate speculation possibilities of the railroad over considerations of traffic and economy of operation. In a number of instances the railroad was built on the outskirts of towns it was intended to serve or some distance from them with the apparent expectation that, as the towns grew, the railroad owners would profit from the resultant real estate activity. The road's construction was not up to prevailing standards or the possibilities of the topography through which it ran with regard to curves and grades. This left something to be desired in terms of economy of operations.

The end result of the conditions described was that the completed railroad did not earn enough to meet operating expenses and its debt obligations. In the fiscal year ending 30 June 1898 capital earnings were $0.685 million and funded debt interest was $1.1 million while for the 1899 fiscal year capital earnings were $0.796. The company was threatened with bankruptcy in early 1899 only a few months after completion to the Gulf. A committee of shareholders was formed in New York in early 1899 to attempt reorganization. This effort did not succeed and in April 1899 the road went into receivership and a new reorganization committee was formed in Philadelphia.

The Kansas City, Pittsburgh & Gulf connected with the Union Pacific at Kansas City and Harriman owned some stock in the former company. As a consequence of these factors, Harriman agreed in April or May of 1899 to join the New York reorganization committee. In November 1899 the Philadelphia reorganization committee gained the support of a majority of the securities and offered a reorganization plan that was adopted. The result was a new company, the Kansas City Southern, which was incorporated in March 1900. Under foreclosures, the new company obtained all the property of the Kansas City, Pittsburgh & Gulf.

During the reorganization discussion Stilwell and his associates sold their interest in the Kansas City, Pittsburgh & Gulf to a group of steel manufacturers headed by John W. Gates. This new group had not previously been involved in railroading. Its members all had holdings in the American Steel & Wire Company of Illinois which had accepted bonds of the Kansas City, Pittsburgh & Gulf in payment for steel rails. Their purchase of control of the road was most likely a means of protecting their interests as creditors and bondholders. Five of this group were among the Kansas City Southern incorporators and four were elected directors and members of the executive committee of that company.

Harriman successfully opposed the initial efforts of Gates and his associates and, as a result, despite the fact that he was a minor stockholder, was elected a director of the reorganized company and chairman of the executive committee. As was commonly done at the time, control of the reorganized property was vested, temporarily, in a board of managers appointed for that purpose known as a "voting trust." The purpose of such trusts was to "avoid the dangers of fluctuating and speculative control of critical periods in a railroad's history . . ." and ". . . that conservative direction be assured until danger of bankruptcy is past."[1] The stockholders of the Kansas City Southern assigned all their powers for a five-year period commencing 1 April 1900 to a voting trust representing about equally Harriman and his associates and Gates and his associates of the American Steel & Wire Company. Among those included in the voting trust were Harriman, Otto Kahn of Kuhn, Loeb & Company, James Stillman of the National City Bank of New York, and George Gould of the Missouri Pacific. Harriman's associates here were also involved with him in the Chicago & Alton as well as in the Union Pacific and Southern Pacific.

The reorganized road had capital stock outstanding of $51 million ($30 million common and $21 million preferred) and funded debt (1st mortgage) of $26.2 million in 3 percent fifty-year bonds compared to $28 million of capital stock and funded debt (1st mortgage) of $22.6 million in 5 percent fifty-year bonds for the Kansas City, Pittsburgh & Gulf. Annual interest on the funded debt was reduced from $1.1 million to $0.786 million as a result of the reorganization, a reduction of 29 percent.

The trustees faced a difficult task. They had an inadequately built and equipped road and they did not have the capital or earnings to quickly bring about the necessary improvements. Under the reorganization plan the new company was supposed to start operations with $3 million in working capital. This did not materialize as the trustees immediately had to provide for the liquidation of car-trust certificates, receivers' certificates, and other prior liens on the Kansas City, Pittsburgh & Gulf totaling $3.25 million. In addition, various betterments authorized or undertaken by the receivers had to be paid. After meeting these various obligations, the trustees had no available cash beyond the capital earnings of the road. During the voting trust period, capital earnings of the road totaled $8 million. Of this sum $5.5 million was spent on betterments and equipment.

From fiscal 1900 to fiscal 1904 (the peak year) capital earnings of the Kansas City Southern rose from $0.733 million to $1.751 million, an increase of 139 percent. This rise in capital earnings provided the wherewithal to make important improvements in the road. It also was the basis for raising the funds needed for further improvements and equipment. Those who took over from the voting trust were able to tap this source of capital and make further significant improvements and equipment additions in a period of rapidly rising prosperity for the railroad.

The voting trust expired on 1 April 1905. Management of the railroad then reverted to the shareholders. As a consequence, control of the Kansas City Southern passed out of the hands of Harriman and Gates. In 1900 Gates and his associates controlled a majority of the shares. Over the years some of the 1900 majority block had reduced their holdings so that the Dutch security holders, combined with some New York interests, controlled the majority of the shares. This group selected a new board of directors at the annual meeting of 17 May 1905. Harriman and Gates offered no opposition. The American representative of the Dutch interests became chairman of the new board of directors which made a sweeping change in the company's officers. Harriman soon thereafter disposed of his interest in the railroad.

The new management, as such are wont to do, painted a dreary picture of the physical condition of the property of which they took control. This was laid at the door of neglect of maintenance under the previous administration. This charge is clearly apple-polishing by the new management. The voting trust had taken over a railroad in very poor condition and during its tenure spent the better part of substantially rising capital earnings on betterments and equipment ($5.5 million out of $8 million). Undoubtedly more remained to be done when 1 April 1905 rolled around. To blame that on neglect of maintenance is far off the mark. Unfortunately, some later writers have accepted this self-serving pronouncement of the new management as the truth. Edward S. Mead in his classic work on corporation finance called the Kansas City Southern an extreme example of the effect of neglect of maintenance upon operating efficiency and upon traffic and earnings. William Z. Ripley (always ready to disparage Harriman) fell for the same story. Ripley wrote that the stockholders of the Kansas City Southern upon coming into possession of their property found it almost completely gutted. Confronted with the facts on investment during the voting trust ($5.5 million), the rise of gross earnings ($4.1 million to $6.6 million or 61 percent), and the increase of capital earnings ($0.733 million to a peak of $1.750 million or 139 percent) during the trust period, such a statement is almost ludicrous. A later statement by Ripley caps this debate. Writing of the benefits to the physical plant of a railroad usually resulting from reorganization, Ripley writes that, "The Kansas City, Pittsburgh & Gulf in 1900 was physically rebuilt and also structurally solidified throughout."[2] What Ripley is referring to was done not in 1900, but was done (or more properly begun) during the voting trust period. The gross contradiction in Ripley's two statements is puzzling. The second is correct and the first quite wrong. There is one possible (and simple) explanation. Hard as it may be to credit, Ripley apparently did not know the Kansas City Southern was the successor to the Kansas City, Pittsburgh & Gulf; that is, he did not know they were one and the same.

Table 8–1 lists the real investment costs and capital earnings of the Kansas City Southern for the years 1900–1909. The years 1906–1909 are included to test how the road did in the period immediately after the end of the voting trust. The internal rate of return during the voting trust period is 4.4 percent. This is low, but represents about a doubling of the prior rate of return. During the voting trust period capital earnings averaged $1.568 million per year versus around $0.7 million in the preceding years. As can be seen from Table 8–1, capital earnings further increased in the years right after the end of the voting trust with the 1906–1909 average rising to $2.77 million. The internal rate of return for 1906–1909 is 8.6 percent, almost double the rate of the voting trust period. For the entire period 1900–1909 the internal rate of return is 5.3 percent.

Gross accounting rates of return are shown in Table 8–2. The difference between the average rate of return is not large, 8.08 percent versus 7.17 percent with this means of viewing the rate of return. The immediate post-voting-trust period is still better than the voting trust period, but not markedly so.

Table 8–1
Kansas City Southern
Investment Cost and Capital Earnings[a]

Year	Investment Costs (000 1900$)	Capital Earnings (000 1900$)
1900	15,718[b]	183.2[c]
1901	0	1,287
1902	5,469[d]	1,625
1903	1,050	1,413
1904	400	1,646
1905	594	1,476
1906	3,948	1,624
1907	2,097	2,987
1908	1,487	2,427
1909	566	2,572

[a]Source: Company reports in the annual volumes of Poor, *Manual of Railroads.*

[b]Kansas City, Pittsburgh & Gulf purchased at foreclosure. The price paid is not available. Estimated on the basis of 60 percent of the par value of Kansas City Southern first mortgage which allows a 5 percent annual yield.

[c]Kansas City Southern began operation 1 April 1900. This is one-quarter of the 30 June 1900 fiscal year total.

[d]Includes purchase of the Kansas City and Independence Air Line, the Union Terminal Railroad Company, and the Kansas City Suburban Belt Railroad Company. Price not available. Valued at 60 percent of the par value of the first mortgages of the acquired lines.

From Table 8–1 it can be seen that the new management engaged in considerable investment in the 1906–1909 period. The current dollar total is $9.1 million. Capital earnings (current dollar) totaled $11.1 million during the period. Investment in betterments and equipment relative to capital earnings was larger in the second period than in the first (82 percent versus 69 percent). However, if we include the 1902 purchases, investment was 98 percent of the capital earnings in the voting trust period.

Table 8–2
Kansas City Southern
Gross Accounting Rates of Return

Year	Gross Capital (000 1900$)	Capital Earnings (000 1900$)	Gross Accounting Rate of Return (%)
1900	15,718	732[a]	4.66
1901	15,718	1,287	8.19
1902	21,187	1,625	7.67
1903	22,237	1,413	6.35
1904	22,637	1,646	7.27
1905	23,231	1,476	6.35
		Mean rate of return	7.17[b]
1906	27,179	1,624	6.00
1907	29,276	2,987	10.20
1908	30,763	2,427	7.89
1909	31,329	2,572	8.21
		Mean rate of return	8.08

[a]Annual rate
[b]Mean for 1901–1905. The railroad only operated three months in 1900 so that year is excluded.

A significant part of the post-voting-trust investment was financed by the issuance of new debt. On 1 November 1905 the sum of $1,440,000 was secured by 4.5 percent ten-year equipment gold notes (Equipment Agreement, Series A) requiring semiannual payments of $72,000. Another $600,000 was obtained 1 June 1906 with 4.5 percent ten-year equipment gold notes (Equipment Agreement, Series B) calling for semi-annual installments of $30,000. On 2 April 1906 a new twenty-year $10 million mortgage (Improvement Mortgage Gold Bonds at 4.5 percent) was executed. Of the $10 million total, $4 million was held in the company treasury. The other $6 million was deposited as security for $5.1 million in six-year collateral trust gold notes issued the same day. The $4 million in improvement mortgage bonds initially withheld were later issued and by 1909 $2.75 million of this amount was spent for various improvements. Of the total, $375,000 was the discount on the bonds and $1,285 million was earmarked for facilities to secure new business and other corporate purposes. These various transactions raised about $10.8 million for equipment, improvements, and repairs. Fixed payments were increased by $552,000 while capital earnings rose by $1.2 million. For conservative finance, an annual sinking fund contributing (with a 5 percent yield) $302,425 would be required to pay off the $10 million mortgage due in 1926. On this conservative basis the net gain in the immediate post-voting-trust period was $346,000 per year, i.e., $1.2 million less ($0.552 million + $0.302 million).

It is also of interest to examine the equipment and productivity records of the Kansas City Southern for 1900–1909. Rolling stock numbers are found in Table 8–3. The output-per-mile figures are presented in Table 8–4. The voting trust management increased locomotives and passenger cars in 1902 and locomotives further in 1904. Locomotives were increased about one-third and passenger cars by 40 percent. The new management invested heavily in rolling stock in 1906 and also added locomotives in 1907 and 1908. The increases were: locomotives, 40 percent; passenger cars, 22 percent; freight cars 15 percent; and service cars, about 50 percent.

Passenger output per mile of road rose 70 percent in the voting trust period while freight output increased one-third. The rise in these figures was maintained in the immediate post-voting-trust period: 66 percent for passenger output and 19 percent for freight output. For all U. S. roads the increases for 1900–1905 were: 25 percent for passenger output and 11 percent for freight; and for 1905–1909: 10 percent for passenger out-

Table 8–3
Kansas City Southern
Rolling Stock[a]

Year	Locomotives	Passenger	Freight	Service
1901	113	48	6,112	549
1902	131	68	5,995	638
1903	130	71	5,872	654
1904	149	70	6,085	471
1905	149	68	5,997	455
1906	168	83	6,918	820
1907	180	83	7,285	665
1908	210	83	7,148	694
1909	208	81	6,908	694

[a]Source: Company reports in annual volumes of Poor, *Manual of Railroads.*

Table 8-4
Kansas City Southern
Passenger and Freight Output Per Mile of Road

Year	Passenger Miles (000)	Freight Ton Miles (000)
1900	24.39	667.34
1901	31.52	685.15
1902	36.43	711.69
1903	38.79	795.91
1904	37.04	882.91
1905	41.42	887.40
1906	47.30	1045.09
1907	67.21	1188.45
1908	67.68	1104.82
1909	68.77	1058.88

[a]Source: Underlying data from company reports in annual volumes of Poor, *Manual of Railroads.*

put and 5 percent for freight. The growth rate of output per mile of road on the Kansas City Southern considerably exceeded the national average in both periods. The U. S. average for passenger miles per mile of road was, however, significantly higher than that of the Kansas City Southern (always a "freight road"): 77.58 versus 41.42 in 1905 and 85.03 compared to 68.77 in 1909. For freight ton miles per mile of road this was reversed with the Kansas City Southern markedly exceeding the national average: 887.40 versus 607.77 in 1905 and 1058.88 compared to 639.12 in 1909.

Productivity growth for the Kansas City Southern exceeded the national average in both periods. To some extent this was the result of the low starting point: the poor condition of the Kansas City, Pittsburgh & Gulf upon foreclosure in 1900. However, it is more than that alone. The average for freight was greater in 1900 than the national average (667.34 versus 547.16). The improvements of *both* the Harriman administration and the succeeding one contributed to this productivity growth performance.

The analysis here indicates that the criticisms of Harriman with regard to the Kansas City Southern are not justified. It is correct that in the immediate post-Harriman period (in part because of what Harriman had done) the road performed better in profitability terms, but in productivity increase its performance was about the same in both periods.

In evaluating Harriman's connection with the Kansas City Southern one should also remember the rather small place it occupied in his affairs. The reconstruction of the Union Pacific and the Southern Pacific, the Burlington and Northern Pacific stock purchases along with the Northern Securities Company and its aftermath, the Chicago & Alton, and the Illinois Central were all far more important. This list doesn't even include other minor activities from the same period. The Kansas City Southern could not have taken much of Harriman's time. It is a little puzzling that it got any. A plausible explanation is that he wanted an additional outlet from Kansas City to the Gulf of Mexico for Union Pacific traffic. He undoubtedly viewed the Kansas City Southern in terms of its strategic value in this traffic. Harriman had a reputation as one of the best railroad men in assessing a road's strategic value. When the Kansas City Southern passed out of his control in 1905 he commissioned a detailed survey and locations of an alternate line from Kansas City to Galveston. Nothing further came of this. Shortly before his last trip to Europe in 1909 an opportunity arose to regain control of the Kansas City Southern and he was said to be giving it serious consideration at the time of his death.

Baltimore & Ohio

Harriman's association with the Baltimore & Ohio coincided with the shifting of control among various interests and an enormous program of reconstruction and reequipment following the railroad's reorganization in 1899. He was elected a director of the Baltimore & Ohio on 17 January 1900 and served on a board that included Jacob Schiff, James Stillman, Norman D. Ream, and James J. Hill.

Executors of the Pullman estate including Philip D. Armour, Marshall Field, and Norman D. Ream, together with James J. Hill bought a larger interest in Baltimore & Ohio stock in September 1898. It was not known whether the interest purchased was sufficient to achieve control. Statements of John K. Cowen, president of the Baltimore & Ohio at the time, suggest that the sale of Baltimore & Ohio stock to this interest group had the goal of gaining the goodwill of railroad men who were strong enough to support the road in case of difficulty, and influential enough to open desirable connections and reduce the stringency of competition. This sounds very much like what Harriman called the achievement of community of interest. The inventor of this type of arrangement among railroad firms, the Pennsylvania Railroad, was soon to become heavily involved in the Baltimore & Ohio and would supplant the "Chicago" group.

Rumors were heard in late 1898 concerning the Pennsylvania's interest in the Balitmore & Ohio and the likelihood of their accuracy was supported by the election of S. M. Prevost, the third vice-president of the Pennsylvania to the Baltimore & Ohio board. This was followed by election of an additional Pennsylvania representative in November 1900.

Hill's interest in the Baltimore & Ohio was substantial. In addition to his stock purchases and service on the board, a further indication of the depth of his interest was the fact that he sent one of his best young men, Frederick D. Underwood, who had made a remarkable record in the construction of the Soo line, to the Balitmore & Ohio to become initially (January 1899) general manager and later (June 1899) its vice-president in charge of operations.

The Chicago group sold its holdings in the Baltimore & Ohio to the Pennsylvania Railroad early in 1901. The financiers reaped a tidy profit on their year-and-a-half holding of the Baltimore & Ohio stock, having purchased it during the receivership for around 26 and selling in the neighborhood of par. Soon after the transfer of control Underwood left the Baltimore & Ohio to become (May 1901) president of the Erie Railroad Company.

After several years of severe financial difficulties associated with the economic downturn of 1893 and succeeding years, the Baltimore & Ohio had gone into receivership in February 1896. One result of the straitened finances of the early nineties was a serious deterioration in the physical capital of the Baltimore & Ohio. The receivers set to work almost immediately to alleviate this condition. About $17 million was spent for cars, $2.5 million for locomotives, $2.1 million for rails, and large sums for improvements and renewals of various kinds so that total investment expenditures by the receivers were around $35 million by 30 June 1899. The receivers surrendered control 1 July 1899.

The task of reconstruction and reequipment of the Baltimore & Ohio started by the receivers was carried forward by the new management and it was this effort in which Harriman was involved. Between the end of receivership and 30 June 1907 about $100 million was spent for equipment and improvements: $17 million from earnings; $15 million from convertible debentures of 1 March 1901; $40 million from new common stock in November 1901; and $28 million from new common stock in 1906. As a consequence, equipment was substantially increased while grades and curvature were reduced, light rails replaced by heavier rails, and multiple track (second, third, and fourth track) and sidings were increased by about one-eighth. Gross earnings of the Baltimore & Ohio grew from $28.4 million in 1899 to $47.1 million in 1901.

Financing the improvements and equipment investment starting in 1899 was aided by the presence on the Baltimore & Ohio board of a phalanx of eminent railroad financiers including William Saloman, James Speyer, Jacob Schiff, Charles Steele, Alexander Brown, and E. H. Harriman. Hill was also there at the start. With the sale of his Baltimore & Ohio stock and the achievement of an absolute majority by the Pennsylvania Railroad, Hill and Charles Tweed, chairman of the Southern Pacific, resigned from the Baltimore & Ohio board in May 1901 and were replaced by two additional representatives of the Pennsylvania. Also in May 1901 John K. Cowen was removed from the presidency of the Baltimore & Ohio by the Pennsylvania on the grounds that an operating man rather than a lawyer should head the Baltimore & Ohio. Cowen's replacement was a distinguished railroad man, Leonor F. Loree, who had been the fourth vice-president of the Pennsylvania lines west of Pittsburgh. The voting trust governing the Baltimore & Ohio was dissolved in August 1901.

What was accomplished in reconstruction and reequipment of the Baltimore & Ohio after 1899 was much the same as Harriman's achievement with the Union Pacific and the Southern Pacific. His contribution apparently also was significant with the Baltimore & Ohio. Underwood specifically gave credit to Harriman for his assistance in raising $32 million for Baltimore & Ohio improvements during Underwood's tenure with the railroad.

Harriman remained on the Baltimore & Ohio board after Hill left, being reelected to the board on 18 November 1901. Given his other ongoing prospects at the time, it is not surprising that his active participation in Baltimore & Ohio affairs ended for several years after 1901. It resumed with the October 1906 purchase of $39,540,600 in Baltimore & Ohio common and preferred stock by the Union Pacific. This large block of stock was purchased from the Pennsylvania which still retained a significant holding in the Baltimore & Ohio. Thus, Harriman contributed to putting the Baltimore & Ohio back in first-class condition and later added this important connector with his roads to the community of interest which he built using the financial muscle provided by the proceeds of the

Northern Securities Company's disposal of its Great Northern and Northern Pacific stock.

Erie Railroad Company

With the hope of bringing the prosperity to southern New York which the Erie Canal was credited with providing for northern New York, the New York & Erie Railroad was organized in 1833. Raising the requisite capital was difficult and not until 1851 did the road finally reach Dunkirk on Lake Erie. A rate war with the New York Central exacerbated the precarious financial situation of the road, and that state of affairs, capped by the effects of the depression starting in 1857, led to a receivership instigated by the holders of the fourth mortgage in August 1859.

In 1861 the reorganization was completed and the road sold in 1862 with the new company incorporated as the Erie Railway Company. The reorganization was an easy one and only a temporary solution to the road's financial problems. Only about $0.5 million of indebtedness was retired and capital stock was increased by a little over $8.9 million of new stock given for floating debt. A 2.5 percent assessment on the new stock provided the means to pay coupons in arrears. Fixed charges were not reduced and no sacrifice was imposed on bondholders. Fortunately, the transportation demands of the Civil War were a tremendous boon to the railroad. This provided the financial underpinning to paper over the weaknesses of the reorganization. The road's western terminus in this period switched from Dunkirk to Buffalo.

The years following the Civil War were a disaster for the Erie. An inland steamboating magnate, Daniel Drew, had gotten on the board of the Erie in 1854 and became treasurer in 1857. James Fisk, Jr. and Jay Gould became close associates of Drew. An earlier steamboating associate of Drew's, Cornelius Vanderbilt, by 1864 had become an influential member of the Erie board. Vanderbilt had the notion of gaining control of the Erie and merging it with the Harlem & Hudson River and the New York Central, which would have given him a virtual railroad monopoly in New York. Vanderbilt did succeed in getting his man, Robert H. Berdell, elected president of the Erie in 1864. His success was short-lived as he was outmaneuvered by Drew who got his associate, Fisk, into the office of vice-president. Drew also in this period began the financial undoing of the Erie as he sold stocks and bonds he found in the Erie treasury (28,000 shares of stock and $4 million in convertible bonds) and brought out a torrent of unauthorized Erie securities. As a consequence of these actions, Drew was thrown out of the Erie. His associate Fisk died from an assassin's bullet on a New York hotel stairway. With Vanderbilt also out, that left Jay Gould who came to the Erie board and became president in late 1868.

Gould's great ambition was to own a single transcontinental railroad. This was a goal toward which he and his son George, who was a sometime associate of Harriman's in various ventures, worked (in the end unsuccessfully while amassing a great fortune) for more than half a century. George was less successful than Jay, a major factor, it is said, being his time-consuming interest in New York chorus girls. Jay Gould's reign at the Erie lasted only until 1872 when he was turned out by General Daniel E. Sickles and his English backers. Gould undertook an ambitious (and severely needed) program of reconstruction and reequipment on the Erie. As a result of the manipulations of Drew and Gould, the bonded indebtedness of the Erie grew from $17.8 million to $26.4 million and common stock from $24.2 million to $78 million between 1864 and 1872. While the bonded indebtedness grew 48 percent and the common stock 221 percent, mileage increased only 53 percent and net earnings but 22 percent. The almost inevitable result was a new receivership which began in May 1875.

The reorganization plan finally adopted was an easy and temporary solution much like the 1861 reorganization. Capitalization of the company would rise by $12 million and fixed charges eventually by $0.5 million. Under average conditions of the past maintenance of solvency was unlikely under this plan and no margin existed for contingencies. Yet the plan was adopted and the property of the Erie Railway sold under foreclosure of the second consolidated mortgage. On 1 June 1878 the new company, the New York, Lake Erie & Western Railroad took possession of the property.

The development of the coal traffic for which it was well located, physical improvement of the road and its equipment, and the attainment of connections with Chicago gave the Erie the appearance of financial health over the next seven years. In 1884 a new crisis arose with unpaid 1 June 1884 coupons of $1 million and other floating debt exceeding $4.4 million. An ingenious scheme was developed to escape these straits without a receivership. However, as Daggett points out, while the ingenuity of the scheme was to be admired, in the end ". . . from any other point of view it was to be condemned as another example of that borrow-

ing to pay interest which had brought the Erie to its existing straits."[3]
The precarious solvency of the Erie was maintained after this latest res-
cue as gross earnings between 1887 and 1892 rose $4.7 million, offset
by a rise of $0.3 million in fixed charges and $4.1 million in operating
expenses.

The thin ice of financial solvency on which it so blithely skated gave
way for the Erie, as it did for so many other railroads, with the onset of
the 1893 economic downturn. On 25 July the company went into
receivership.

In 1893 Harriman happened to have a small holding of Erie second-
mortgage, 6 percent bonds. On 1 January 1894 a reorganization plan was
put forward backed by the well-known firms of Drexel, Morgan & Company of New York and J. S. Morgan & Company of London. This plan
suffered from weaknesses similar to those of the two previous Erie reorganizations. There was to be no assessment on stockholders, no syndicate to raise money, and no voting trust. The second consolidated and
other junior bondholders were to be forced to subscribe to a new bond
issue that in the end would again raise fixed charges. In general, the effect of the plan was to make an assessment on the road's (junior) creditors for the benefits of those who owned its equity.

Harriman was joined in his objections to the reorganization plan by
Kuhn, Loeb & Company, August Belmont, Vermilye & Company, Hall-
garten & Company, and Charles Peabody (representing the Astor estate).
A letter of objection from the bondholders protective committee headed
by Harriman was sent to the Erie's directors and ignored by them. A
meeting of stockholders (not very surprisingly) approved the plan on 6
March, and Drexel, Morgan & Company, having received deposits of a
majority of each class of bond, gave notice that the plan would be oper-
ative as announced. Harriman (joined by others) filed suit in the U. S.
Supreme Court for an injunction to prevent the recording of the new
mortgage. This was denied on the grounds that no legal right of the minority holders had been endangered.

Harriman's apparent defeat on this issue was reversed by the weakness
of the plan itself. In June and December 1894 coupon payments then due
could not be made. The result was the enforced abandonment of the plan
and the adoption in August 1895 of a quite different plan that met many
of the objections raised by Harriman and others. The new and final plan
put the burden of readjustment on both stocks and bonds instead of bonds
alone. The new plan lowered rather than raised fixed charges, and it pro-

cured cash from stockholders rather than from second consolidated mortgage holders. This third reorganization for the first time corrected the ills of previous reorganizations and gave some promise of financial solvency for the Erie. While the force of circumstance was a major factor in this outcome, Harriman's participation in and leadership of the opposition also contributed to the Erie's movement toward a sounder financial base. After the reorganization, the Erie shared in the prosperity of the country with its gross revenue between 1895 and 1907 rising from $31.5 million to $53.9 million. Its position was still not assured since in 1907, out of the largest income it ever received, the road paid out 89 percent for operating expenses, fixed charges, and taxes.

Harriman was brought into greater prominence in the field of railroad finance by this second conflict with Morgan. Leading bankers and brokerage houses came to hold a higher opinion of his abilities and judgment. This would be beneficial in his great works which at this point lay just ahead of him.

As a security holder (and resident on its line) Harriman maintained an interest in the management of the Erie Railroad Company as the firm was known after the 1895 reorganization. Following Underwood's election as president in 1901, Harriman expressed an interest in becoming a director of the Erie. While he had a good relationship with Underwood at the Baltimore & Ohio, the renewal of that relationship was probably not, as Harriman's biographer writes, the primary reason for his desire to sit on the Erie board. A further broadening of the community of interest involving his railroads was undoubtedly the main goal. On 30 September 1903 Harriman was elected to the Erie board and on 28 June 1905 he became a member of the executive committee. In these positions he was instrumental in raising the $5 million necessary to build two subsidiary roads, the Erie & Jersey and the Genesee River, extensions which were designed to reduce grades and to relieve congestion on the New York and Allegheny divisions of the Erie.

One area where Harriman's influence, ability, and financial experience were particularly helpful to the Erie between 1903 and 1906 was in the question of equipment and improvements. Despite the Erie's limited resources and impaired credit, Harriman always voted in favor of better equipment and improvements. He emphatically objected to one director's proposal to cease altogether, for a time, the making of equipment purchases. His motto was that, "The way to save money is to spend it."[4] By this he did not mean that money should be squandered, but that it should be spent freely when it would increase earning power. Harriman's contribution to the Erie in this respect was widely recognized. In 1916 *Railway Age Gazette* wrote with respect to the Erie's rebuilding,

The Erie unquestionably owes to Mr. Harriman and his immediate associates much, as regards the breadth and scope of the plan of rehabilitation and the tenacity with which it was adhered to under the most trying circumstances.[5]

The panic and business depression of 1907 brought the Erie once again to the doorstep of receivership. For years the company had met obligations by issuing short-term notes. The depression made renewal of short-term obligations difficult. The Erie had $5.5 million in such notes maturing 8 April 1908. The plan was to issue $15 million in new notes maturing in three years with interest at 6 percent. The $15 million was to be divided as follows: $5.5 million exchanged for those due 8 April 1908, $5 million sold at par the remainder reserved for future use. J. P. Morgan & Company agreed to underwrite $5 million of the new notes if the holders of the old notes exchanged old for new at par. However, the latter would not make the exchange and J. P. Morgan & Company was not willing both to take up the old notes and assume the risk of the new issue. Receivership appeared inevitable. A conference was set up for the evening of 7 April in J. P. Morgan's library.

Besides his feelings as a director of the Erie, Harriman was concerned that receivership for the Erie would precipitate a new Wall Street panic causing failure of other companies and prolongation of the business recession. Several members of Morgan's firm, directors of the Erie including Harriman, and other financiers were present for the meeting in Morgan's library. After considerable discussion Harriman offered to furnish half the $5.5 million if other interested parties would come up with the remainder. After a long separate consultation the other parties announced their unwillingness to put up any part of the funds. Harriman then offered to put up the entire amount if the other parties would lend it to him. This too was refused and the meeting broke up in the early hours of 8 April after it was agreed to delay filing the receivership temporarily. By the next day Harriman had decided to put up the entire amount, which he was able to borrow from the National City Bank. His only condition was that Underwood was to remain as president of the Erie until the loan was paid.

When news of Harriman's actions became known, the stock market rallied strongly with Erie stocks leading the way. Harriman's role was widely recognized by the financial world and eventually the general public. This action was a major cause of the improvement of his public image during the remainder of his life. The *Commercial and Financial Chronicle* wrote,

> Mr. Harriman has saved the Erie road from a receivership. In doing so he has taken a heavy load off the market and ought to receive the gratitude of the public.[6]

In a similar vein the *Financial World* said,

> Harriman's rescue of the Erie, when its own bankers had apparently deserted it, will long be remembered as a master stroke of courage and resourcefulness, which saved not only the Erie, but the general financial situation from serious embarrassment.[7]

Summary

Compared to his great endeavors, especially those with the Illinois Central, the Union Pacific, and the Southern Pacific, Harriman's association and activities with the Kansas City Southern, the Baltimore & Ohio, and the Erie were minor plays indeed. However, in each case we can see his overriding concern with efficiency and careful financial management. The same goals guided his participation in the minor as in the great dramas representing his major achievements. Moreover, in the instance of the Erie in 1908 we see another side of Harriman not so clearly visible. That was a concern for the public interest over and above that of a particular company and his own personal interest. In the final reckoning this consideration must receive its appropriate place.

CHAPTER NINE

Under Attack:
The ICC Investigation 1906–1907

About the time Harriman was preparing to attend the Dubuque & Sioux City Railroad Company stockholders meeting at Dubuque in early 1887 an event occurred in Washington, D. C. that was to have a major impact on his later years and career. The Act to Regulate Commerce (the Interstate Commerce Act) was passed to bring all railroads engaged in interstate commerce under federal control in order to maintain competitive conditions. The Interstate Commerce Commission (ICC) was created to oversee the regulatory process initiated by the Act. The basic provisions of the act were (a) that railroad rates must be "just" and "reasonable"; (b) the outlawing of personal discrimination with regard to rates; (c) forbidding undue preference to any shipper, place, or kind of traffic; (d) the prohibition of greater charges "for transportation of passengers or of like kind of property, under substantially similar circumstances and conditions, for a shorter than for a longer distance, over the same line, in the same direction, the shorter being included in the longer distance"; (e) pooling agreements were made illegal; and (f) railroads were required to publish fares and rates for everyone's information and could not change fares or rates without ten days notice. The Commission was required by the Act to (a) look into the business of the railroads; (b) hear complaints on alleged violations of the Act and issue "cease and desist" orders on findings of unlawful practices; (c) require railroads to issue annual reports based on a uniform system of accounts; and(d) submit an annual report to Congress.

The law and the associated charge to the ICC was broad enough to give the Commission generous leeway in its activities. This open-endedness was taken advantage of in the investigation involving Harriman. Officially the ICC investigation begun in 1906 was an inquiry into "The Consolidation and Combination of Carriers." Under shelter of this broad and innocuous title the Commission's investigation was in fact rather limited and sharply pointed. From the title one could easily envisage a wide-ranging investigation looking at all those railroads involved in consolidation and presumably combination. On the other hand, a moment's reflection should suggest that such an investigation would be nonsense since every major road in the country represented to some extent or other the processes of consolidation and combination. And in fact, of course, the 1906 investigation was not nearly so broad or wide-ranging as implied by its somewhat grandiose title. First, the investigation was restricted by geography, in this case to primarily western roads. Second, it was also restricted rather specifically to those railroads that were controlled or had been managed at some time by E. H. Harriman. As his biographer correctly points out, the inquiry should have been entitled "An Investigation of the so-called Harriman Lines."

It is easy enough to see why the "Harriman" railroads might have excited the attention of a regulatory agency with the law to enforce and the charge provided to the ICC. First, through his control of the Union Pacific and the Southern Pacific, Harriman controlled two of the three central and southern transcontinental routes. This pretty clearly would give him the whip hand with respect to the transcontinental traffic of a significant segment of the nation. In addition, the Union Pacific was a strong competitor for the transcontinental traffic of the Pacific Northwest. However, here there were two (or three if one counts the Burlington) other competitors (alternatives). Concern about the abuse of competition should have been much less with regard to Pacific Northwest traffic.

In addition to concern about competition in the markets directly served by the Harriman roads, the regulatory fever also could have been raised by the outcome of the Northern Securities case which we examined above. That result, it will be recalled, was to give the Union Pacific (and therefore Harriman) a large stake in the ownership of several major railroads with which the Union Pacific was either a competitor (the Atchison, Topeka & Santa Fe) or directly or indirectly a connector (the

Baltimore & Ohio, the Chicago, Milwaukee & St. Paul, the Chicago & Northwestern, the Illinois Central, and the New York Central). This is a rather impressive list of United States railroads (especially when we add the Union Pacific and the Southern Pacific to it) over which one person was in a position to exercise control. It is easy to see why the regulatory mentality would be aroused by such a litany.

Given the potential concerns described, the really surprising thing about the ICC investigation is that its major focus was not on those issues of competition but instead on the relatively insignificant matter of the Chicago & Alton reorganization. If one is concerned about maintenance of competition and reduction in the exercise of monopoly power, the Chicago & Alton seems a frail rod on which to unleash the lightning (and thunder) of regulatory power. The grandly named ICC investigation was thus restricted both geographically and personally, and its primary emphasis was not even the obvious targets of regulatory displeasure. The Chicago & Alton involved some consolidation. What railroad out of the very minor leagues did not? The Chicago & Alton didn't have much in the way of combination. Under Blackstone, the Chicago & Alton had ignored or spurned a number of potential consolidations that would have greatly strengthened it in the last two decades of the nineteenth century. The thinking of the Chicago & Alton's management is illustrated by the proud annual anouncements in the nineties of the growing percentage of its business that was "local." Over the first half of the twentieth century the Chicago & Alton had a succession of suitors, but it found no long-term mate until after World War II when the Gulf, Mobile & Ohio finally succeeded where so many others had failed. As Albro Martin had so aptly put it, the Chicago & Alton was one of the most troublesome "old maids" in the entire family of midwestern railroads. In 1906 it should not have been a cause for concern about consolidation and combination, unless the concern was how to get it further consolidated or combined so that it could operate more efficiently.

Harriman was an obvious target. Yet there were other fish in the sea. Why was Harriman selected? George Kennan, Albro Martin, and Jonathan Hughes all conclude that the reason was the animus held against Harriman by the rough rider in the White House. The available evidence supports this view. Roosevelt and Harriman had been on friendly terms for years. Harriman was often invited to the White House, addressed as "My dear Mr. Harriman," and consulted about various matters. These friendly relations were broken off in the fall of 1906 apparently due to a misunderstanding about what was said or meant in a discussion at the White House shortly before the 1904 election.

Roosevelt had written Harriman in June of 1904 to see him when he (Harriman) returned from Europe. Harriman on 20 September, upon returning from Europe, wrote offering to see Roosevelt at any time. A few days later Roosevelt wrote Harriman including the statement that, "At present there is nothing to see you about. . . ."[1] This was followed on 10 October by another request from Roosevelt for Harriman to come and see him, and another acceptance by Harriman. The trouble apparently was fund-raising for the Republican party in New York and the consequent concern that not only the Republican candidate for governor would be defeated but possibly also Roosevelt himself. Having received Harriman's acceptance, Roosevelt then wrote on 14 October a very strange letter which assumes that the invitation was not accepted, that Harriman doubted the wisdom of accepting it, and that if Harriman's reluctance to refuse a direct request from the president were overcome he would stay in New York.

A plausible explanation for this turn of events is that Roosevelt decided that Harriman's prominence as a railroad man and capitalist made it politically dangerous to seem to seek his help. Given its later use, it appears that Roosevelt's second letter was intended to be a "letter of record" available for later proof that the visit was initiated by Harriman and that he was seeking the president's aid for his own purposes. In fact, the letter was later used for precisely this purpose by Roosevelt in testimony before a Senate investigating committee.

Harriman and Roosevelt had a conference at the White House on 20 October. The outcome was that Harriman went back to New York and raised $250,000 (himself giving $50,000) for the Republican National Committee. He also received Roosevelt's promise that Senator Depew of New York would be appointed ambassador to France, leaving the Senate race for Governor Black and removing a divisive contest in New York. In December Harriman had a short talk with Roosevelt in Washington in which the latter told him he did not think it necessary to appoint Depew and that he favored his reelection to the Senate. Harriman was disturbed by this going back on a promise but believed that it was due to misunderstanding.

In the fall of 1906 the Republican party was again short of funds and Harriman was solicited for a contribution which he refused to make. The chairman of the Republican Congressional Committee, James S. Sherman, reported on the interview with Harriman to Roosevelt a few days later. Roosevelt then (8 October 1906) wrote Sherman a letter of record in which he denied having promised Depew's appointment as ambassador and went on to say:

So much for what Mr. Harriman said about me personally. Far more important are the additional remarks he made to you, as you inform me, when you asked him if he thought it well for Hearstism and the like to triumph over the Republican Party. You inform me that he told you that he did not care in the least; because these people were crooks and he could buy them; and whenever he wanted legislation from a state legislature he could buy it; that he "could buy Congress," and that if necessary, "he could buy the judiciary." This was doubtless said partly in boastful cynicism and partly in a mere burst of bad temper because of his objection to the Interstate Commerce Law and to my actions as President. But it shows a cynicism and deep-seated corruption which makes the man uttering such sentiments, and boasting, no matter how falsely, of his power to perform such crimes, at least as undesirable a citizen as Debs, or Moyer, or Haywood.[2]

Fortunately a third person, Maxwell Evarts, Harriman's legal counsel, was present during the conversation between Harriman and Sherman that Roosevelt related in his letter to Sherman. Evarts states that in the conversation Harriman rather brusquely told Sherman that he was not going to make a campaign contribution and that he could use his money better elsewhere. Nothing was said about buying legislatures, courts, etc. In December 1906 Harriman, apparently having heard about Roosevelt's letter to Sherman, had Evarts see Roosevelt and tell him about the conversation with Sherman. Thus, Roosevelt knew as early as December 1906 that the representations made to him by Sherman about the Harriman conversation were false. Despite this, in April 1907 Roosevelt gave his letter to Sherman to the press for publication.

It may, as Roosevelt claimed, have been only coincidence, but the ICC investigation of the Harriman lines was begun in November 1906, almost two months after Roosevelt's letter to Sherman. Opinion in the Roosevelt administration concerning an investigation of the Harriman lines was apparently mixed. Attorney General Bonaparte, Secretary of War Taft, Frank B. Kellogg (general counsel of the ICC), and Franklin K. Lane, a member of the ICC, supported such an investigation while Elihu Root and Martin A. Knapp of the ICC opposed it. It was Bonaparte who in March 1907 initiated the effort to seek dissolution of the Union

Pacific–Southern Pacific tie and challenge the Union Pacific's 30 percent ownership of the Illinois Central.

The Investigation

The ICC initiated its investigation entitled "In the Matter of Consolidations and Combinations of Carriers, Relations Between Such Carriers, and Community of Interests Therein, Their Rates, Facilities and Practices" on 15 November 1906. The investigation focused heavily on certain transactions of the Union Pacific Railroad Company with special emphasis on the acquisition of control of the Southern Pacific Company but also, disproportionately, on the Chicago & Alton reorganization.

The first section of the Commission's report deals with "The Harriman Policy." A recitation of the reorganization of the Union Pacific and the restructuring of its system is given. The principal conclusion drawn is that the policies and purposes of the Union Pacific were those of Harriman. One cannot quarrel with that conclusion since it is clear from the record that such was the case.

The "Harriman Policy" is stated by the Commission to be in control of all existing transcontinental lines, or as many as possible, and to exclude the entry of all competitors. This is supported by a recitation of the expanse of rail and steamship lines controlled by Harriman and by his testimony before the Commission. In that testimony Harriman stated that in essence the antitrust law was all that kept him from adding additional railroads to those he already controlled.

It is very illuminating that the Commission, not by any means friendly to Harriman and his interests, wrote with regard to Harriman's policy that:

It has been, however, no part of the Harriman policy to permit the properties which were brought under the Union Pacific control to degenerate or decline; as railroads they are better properties today, with lower grades, straighter tracks, and more ample equipment than they were when they came under that control. Large sums have been generously expended in the carrying on of engineering works and betterments which make for the improvement of the service and the permanent value of the property.[3]

With respect to the Southern Pacific, the Commission demonstrates the extent of Union Pacific control, including Harriman's admission that the Union Pacific controlled the Southern Pacific. The important point to the

Commission is that in unifying the two properties and exercising control over the Southern Pacific, the Union Pacific ". . . has effected a substantial elimination of competition between two lines." The Commission's argument is that before the Union Pacific acquired control of the Southern Pacific there was competition between the two for transcontinental traffic. It is admitted that this competition was not as complete as it might have been if the Union Pacific had had its own line into San Francisco rather than being dependent on the Central Pacific. One interesting point the Commission makes with regard to this competition is that, prior to the Southern Pacific acquisition, rates for traffic bound to the Pacific Coast from the Atlantic seaboard east of Buffalo and Pittsburgh were identical no matter what route was taken. This is rather strange evidence for competition. The Commission by "competition" presumably had the layman's notion of competition in mind, the competition of oligopolies and so on. Price for each producer would be the same under the economist's notion of competition, i.e., perfect competition, but this would result because the firms were price-takers merely accepting the price set for them by the market. Railroads are not price-takers. Presumably the Commission thought that without competition rates will differ by route. One wonders why the public would necessarily be better off when everyone charges the same rate. The consolidation of the Union Pacific and Southern Pacific steamship lines is also alleged to have destroyed all competition between those lines.

The Commission makes a great deal, under the heading "Considerations of National Policy," of the legal requirement for the Central Pacific to form a through line with the Union Pacific. It is stated that while the Central Pacific is undoubtedly a desirable acquisition for the Union Pacific, such acquisition was not necessary because of the legal requirement cited. This argument overlooks two points. First, the physical condition and capacity of the Central Pacific relative to the Union Pacific is not considered. As we saw earlier, the Central Pacific was a serious bottleneck for the Union Pacific in that the full benefits to the Union Pacific of its improvement and reconstruction could not be enjoyed by itself or the public unless the Central Pacific was reconstructed in a similar fashion— as it was under Harriman's control. Second, while there was a legal requirement for the Central Pacific and Union Pacific together to maintain a through road, there was no constraint requiring the lessees of the Central Pacific (the Southern Pacific Company) to ship over that line. There were clear gains to them by utilizing the Sunset Route rather than the Central Pacific-Union Pacific line. The relative efficiency of the two alternates did not necessarily determine the route chosen. These two problems were largely resolved from the point of view of the Union Pacific (and also to a certain extent from society's viewpoint) by the effective merger of the Union Pacific and Central Pacific. The Commission certainly did not, contrary to its apparent belief, establish that the merger was inimical to the public welfare or "considerations of national policy."

The Commission undertook a detailed examination and recitation of the Union Pacific's stock ownership in other railroads which we discussed in chapter 6. It was also specifically concerned about the joint ownership arrangement worked out with the San Pedro, Los Angeles & Salt Lake Railroad. The Commission maintained that this arrangement reduced competition because an independent San Pedro, Los Angeles & Salt Lake with a Salt Lake connection to the Denver & Rio Grande-Missouri Pacific system would have made in effect two new overland routes from Los Angeles to the Mississippi River. With regard to Union Pacific ownership of stock in other railroads, the Commission makes no direct allegations regarding competition, but from the tenor of the discussion it seems clear that the Commission disapproved of such ownership and believed it to be against public interest.

Out of a thirty-page report on its investigation, the Commission spent eight full pages on the Chicago & Alton (included in pages 295–303 of the report). This more than anything else vividly demonstrates the bias of the Commission and makes plausible the assertion that the investigation was a hunting expedition aimed at unearthing some criminal charge against Roosevelt's "undesirable citizen" and "enemy of the Republic." There should have been little in the Chicago & Alton affair to excite the Commission's concern about competition, although there is some discussion of this in the report concerning the Union Pacific's ownership (control) of the Illinois Central which was a competing road to the Chicago & Alton. The excuse given for the Commission's inquiry into the reorganization and capitalization of the Chicago & Alton is the Union Pacific's 1903 purchase of 103,431 shares of preferred stock of the Chicago & Alton Railway Company.

The Commission's report raises all the bromides about the Chicago & Alton that we examined in chapter 7. In the beginning an attempt is made to paint the Chicago & Alton in a favorable light by the statement that prior to 1898 the Chicago & Alton under the control of T. B. Blackstone had paid an average dividend of 8 percent per year and "in addition had expended large sums out of earnings in the improvement of its property.'' So far as can be determined from the company reports the latter statement is simply wrong. Edward S. Mead, writing in 1910, noted that the condition of the Chicago & Alton in the 1890s was far below that of its competitors and its property had not been kept up to standard. The Chicago & Alton earned about $2.7 million on average per year between 1893 and 1898. An 8 percent dividend on outstanding stock would require two-thirds of this sum ($1.8 million) each year. Moreover, a total of $770,777 in fixed charges was due in 1899 (see Table 7–8) and approximately that sum for the period cited. Thus, it would appear that dividends and fixed payments required about $2.6 million out of 2.7 million in earnings. Even if all the remainder (about $0.1 million) were spent on improvements, that is hardly a ''large sum.'' The Commission neglected to point out with respect to the large dividend payments that one-third of the Chicago & Alton stock was owned by Blackstone. Rather than the favorable view of the Commission, what we really find for the Chicago & Alton in the nineties is a railroad paying large dividends with its president owning a substantial portion of the stock and neglecting the maintenance of its physical capital.

The Commission's conclusion was that the Harriman syndicate's financing of the Chicago & Alton was indefensible. The Commission also attempted to demonstrate that the road was run down after Harriman's control. Both of these allegations are dealt with in more detail in chapter 7. Suffice it to say here that they are both unfounded. The Commission was forced to note that dividends and interest payments totaled about $2.8 million annually under the Blackstone administration compared to fixed payments of $3.5 million under the new capitalization. In this regard the Commission wrote,

The plan adopted was to substitute long-term bonds and guaranteed stock bearing an exceptionally low rate of interest for common stock which paid a large dividend and for bonds about to mature bearing a high rate of interest. Thus the property was not burdened with an interest payment proportionate to the increase in capitalization, no matter how great the profits made from reorganization.[4]

What the Commission describes appears to be a perfectly reasonable (and clever) bit of financing. The profits arose from the financing and may be viewed as the reward for the application of intelligence and skill. As is so frequently the case, those who are not so intelligent and skillful begrudge the reward to those who are their betters in these matters. The important point in this (which the Commission did not make) was that the Chicago & Alton got a capital infusion of around $15 million for an additional $.7 million in charges, a cost of about 4.6 percent.

The Commission's overall conclusions dealt with the issue of competition. It concluded that the combined operation of the Union Pacific and Southern Pacific had eliminated competition between them in transcontinental business and in business to and from the Orient. The joint ownership of San Pedro, Los Angeles & Salt Lake Railroad was also said to have eliminated competition. Union Pacific ownership of Santa Fe stock was judged to have eliminated competition between those roads. The result of these ownership changes was viewed as especially deleterious to the Denver & Rio Grande system, causing it to lose business and eliminating another transcontinental rival. The joint control of the Chicago & Alton by the Union Pacific and the Chicago, Rock Island & Pacific Railway Company was seen as eliminating competition between the Chicago & Alton and Rock Island. The final word by way of conclusion was that, "If the policy of purchasing and controlling stocks in competing lines is permitted to continue, it must mean suppression of competition."

The Commission made three recommendations in the report, as follows:

1. The function of a railroad corporation should be confined to the furnishing of transportation. Railroads should not be permitted to invest generally in the stock, bonds, and securities of other railways and of steamship companies, except connecting lines.

2. It is contrary to public policy, as well as unlawful, for railways to acquire control of parallel and competing lines. . . . ownership of any stock by one railway company in a competing railway should not be permitted, and such lines of railway should be prohibited from having any common directors or officers.

3. The time has come when some reasonable regulation should be imposed upon the issuance of securities by railways engaged in interstate commerce. [Old established railway systems with good credit] should be prevented from inflating their securities for merely speculative purposes. Reasonable regulation will tend to make them [railroad securities] safe and more secure investments, and thereby benefit not only the railway companies but the public.[5]

In the Commission's eyes Harriman was guilty of operating contrary to each of these recommendations. The Commission obviously viewed this with disfavor and sought to prevent such actions in the future.

Of these three recommendations, the second was on the soundest footing. It already was in fact the law. Of course, its precise application might appear differently to people of good intentions and honor. Harriman understood that control of competing lines was illegal. He apparently did not believe the Southern Pacific was a true competitor, and in fact that was the argument of the Union Pacific's lawyers when the government's case for dissolution of the Union Pacific and the Southern Pacific got to court. This all ignores the problem of the Central Pacific's condition. It was imperative by 1901 that the Central Pacific be rebuilt either by its present owners (who weren't doing it and showed no inclination to do so) or by Harriman after purchasing it, and the present owners weren't selling the Central Pacific by itself. One could make a plausible case that the Southern Pacific Company's not rebuilding the Central Pacific and not selling it to Harriman were themselves actions designed to stifle competition, that is, Collis P. Huntington, who led the ownership group of the Southern Pacific, was the one guilty of holding down competition. Harriman got around this obstacle by buying the Southern Pacific Company. The trouble with general rules like that embodied in the second recommendation is that they may not apply or be best for society in every case. That was exactly the case for the Union Pacific's purchase of control of the Southern Pacific.

The first and third recommendations are more dubious than the second. Certainly Harriman's railroads (as did all other major railroads) did more than just provide transportation. It is very hard to see how society would be placed on a higher plane of well-being by the implementation of the first recommendation. The third recommendation is even more troublesome. What exactly is meant by "inflating their securities merely for speculative purposes"? Few would deny that some control of security issuance and security markets has benefits for society. Since the Securities and Exchange Act of 1934 we have such protection in law for securities in general, not only railroad securities. In the Chicago & Alton reorganization the Commission felt that Harriman had inflated securities for speculative purposes. In general the Commission's conclusions about the Chicago & Alton financing are wide of the mark. Basing a recommendation on such flawed analysis is on shaky ground indeed.

Rate Performance of the Harriman Roads

Since the Commission was so concerned about the issue of competition with regard to the Harriman roads, it is of interest to examine their rates. We will review and compare rates for passengers and freight, which are simply revenue per passenger mile and per freight ton mile, for the major Harriman lines and the U. S. average. Unfortunately these averages, like all averages, leave a lot to be desired. For example, the average rate per ton mile for freight depends not only on the level of rates for various classes of traffic, but also on a number of other factors. An important determinant of the average is the distribution of classes of traffic. Suppose we are comparing two railroads with identical freight ton miles for a given year. Different classes of traffic have different levels of freight rate. Imagine only two classes of traffic, say, coal and finished goods. If one road had half its ton miles in coal and the other only one third of its ton miles in coal, the first will have a lower average ton rate. Does this mean the second road is overpriced or less efficient than the first? The answer is obviously no.

If an average rate is for a railroad system, and in general that is the only information one can get for long periods of time, the mere difference in composition of the systems between main line and branch lines could produce different rates. This point can be illustrated by the Union Pacific for 1899. The length of the system in that year was 5,399 miles composed of the Union Pacific itself (2,855 miles), the Oregon Railroad & Navigation Company (1,063 miles), and the Oregon Short Line (1,481 miles). Average 1899 freight rate per ton mile for these roads, respectively, in cents per ton mile was: 1.015; 1.538; and 0.91 while average rate per passenger mile in cents for 1899 was 1.979; 2.788; and 2.69. Note that the Navigation Company's rates are highest for both passengers and freight. The result is to make the Union Pacific system average significantly higher than that of the main stem. In 1899 the system average for freight is 1.09 cents per ton mile compared to 1.015 for the Union Pacific. For passengers the gap is larger because the Oregon Short Line is also much higher than the Union Pacific (rather than lower as in the case of freight) so that the system average is 2.33 cents per passenger mile compared to the Union Pacific's 1.979 cents per passenger mile. The relatively low traffic density of the Navigation Company and Oregon Short Line routes had much to do with their relatively high rates.

For the reasons noted, among others, direct comparison of average rates requires a great deal of caution. In general, it is better to look at changes over time when using average rates rather than comparing the levels themselves at a point in time. Of course, changes in the distribution of freight by class and alterations in the breakdown of system mileage between main line and branches can change over time and produce a change in average rate over time even though everything else is constant. The impact over time of the changes cited is likely to be less of a problem for comparison of changes in rates over time between railroads (systems) than the effect of the factors cited in comparison of the levels of rates between railroads at a point in time.

Another consideration necessary when one compares freight and passenger rates over time is the change in the price level. This requires that comparisons be made in real terms rather than nominal terms. In what follows here both nominal and real rates are shown, but our discussion focuses on the real and, for the reasons cited above, on changes over time. The Bureau of Labor Statistics wholesale price index used earlier is employed to convert from current to real terms.

Table 9–1 presents average freight rates for the principal Harriman lines (the Union Pacific, Southern Pacific, and Illinois Central) and for all U. S. roads. The following discussion is of the real (1900$) rates. The Union Pacific shows a relatively high rate in 1899, but this drops sharply in 1900 and generally continues to decline thereafter. The Southern Pacific series is more nearly constant, showing some decline after 1901, but not so much as the Union Pacific. The Union Pacific rates lie below the Southern Pacific in every year after 1901. The average ton

Table 9–1
Revenue per Freight Ton Mile[a]
(¢)

Year	Union Pacific Current $	Union Pacific 1900$	Southern Pacific Current $	Southern Pacific 1900$	Illinois Central Current $	Illinois Central 1900$	All U.S. Roads Current $	All U.S. Roads 1900$
1899	1.09	1.17	.95	1.02	.69	.74	.72	.78
1900	.96	.96	.98	.98	.65	.65	.73	.73
1901	1.00	1.01	1.00	1.01	.62	.63	.75	.76
1902	.98	.93	1.02	.97	.62	.59	.76	.72
1903	.96	.90	1.02	.96	.59	.56	.76	.72
1904	.97	.91	1.01	.95	.61	.57	.78	.73
1905	.89	.83	1.05	.98	.59	.55	.77	.72
1906	.91	.83	1.02	.93	.56	.51	.75	.68
1907	.96	.83	1.10	.95	.58	.50	.76	.65
1908	1.00	.89	1.10	.98	.59	.53	.75	.67
1909	1.03	.85	1.15	.95	.60	.50	.76	.63

[a]Data for all U.S. roads from *Historical Statistics of the United States* (series Q312 and Q345). For the individual railroads the data is from company reports in annual volumes of Poor, *Manual of Railroads*. System averages for the Union Pacific are not provided for 1899–1901 and are estimated from available information.

mile rates for the Illinois Central and all U. S. roads follow the same general pattern over the time period as those for the Union Pacific and the Southern Pacific. Both of the former are lower in absolute level of average rate than the latter. The Illinois Central average rate in absolute terms is markedly lower than that for all U. S. roads.

What about changes over time? Take 1901 (the year Harriman acquired the Southern Pacific) as the starting point. In 1901 the average freight rate was identical for the Union Pacific and the Southern Pacific. Between 1901 and 1909 the Union Pacific average rate falls 16 percent compared to 6 percent for the Southern Pacific, 21 percent for the Illinois Central, and 17 percent for all U. S. roads. The declines of the Union Pacific and U. S. average are essentially identical while the Illinois Central falls significantly more rapidly and the Southern Pacific much less rapidly.

Table 9–2 provides average passenger mile rates. Again, the following discussion deals with the real rates. The general time pattern of average passenger mile rates is similar to that for average freight rates. One difference is that the Southern Pacific is quite close to (and in the last three years lower) than the Union Pacific rather than being higher as in the

Table 9–2
Revenue per Passenger Mile[a]
(¢)

Year	Union Pacific Current $	1900$	Southern Pacific Current $	1900$	Illinois Central Current $	1900$	All U.S. Roads Current $	1900$
1899	2.33	2.51	2.25	2.42	2.014	2.17	1.978	2.127
1900	2.23	2.23	2.18	2.18	2.021	2.021	2.003	2.003
1901	2.24	2.27	2.28	2.31	1.960	1.99	2.013	2.042
1902	2.25	2.14	2.20	2.10	1.999	1.90	1.986	1.891
1903	2.16	2.03	2.18	2.05	1.971	1.86	2.006	1.891
1904	2.15	2.02	2.14	2.01	1.970	1.85	2.006	1.885
1905	2.14	2.00	2.18	2.04	1.839	1.72	1.962	1.832
1906	2.06	1.87	2.24	2.03	1.956	1.77	2.003	1.818
1907	2.19	1.88	2.11	1.82	1.963	1.69	2.014	1.733
1908	2.19	1.95	2.17	1.94	1.857	1.66	1.937	1.728
1909	2.22	1.84	2.18	1.81	1.836	1.52	1.928	1.600

[a]Data for all U.S. roads from *Historical Statistics of the United States* (series Q312 and Q345). For the individual railroads the data is from company reports in annual volumes of Poor, *Manual of Railroads.* System averages for the Union Pacific are not provided for 1899–1901 and are estimated from available information.

case of average freight rates. With 1901 as the base, the Union Pacific average passenger rate falls 19 percent by 1909 compared to a decline of 22 percent for the Southern Pacific, 24 percent for the Illinois Central, and 22 percent for all U. S. roads. For all intents and purposes, these declines are identical. Properly viewed, the performance of the Harriman roads in terms of the movement of average passenger rates over time was identical over the period 1901–1909. Moreover, the performance of these roads was identical, on average, to that of all U. S. roads.

Subject to the qualifications cited earlier, the behavior of average freight and passenger rates for the Harriman roads over the 1901–1909 period does not provide support for the concern of the ICC regarding the competitive impact of Harriman's actions. The decline in real rates is significant except in the case of freight for the Southern Pacific. With the exception noted, the public was gaining as much or more from the movements of average rates for the Harriman roads as it was for all U. S. roads on average. The Commission's concern about Harriman's impact on competition appears to have been rather considerably overdrawn.

The decline in railroad rates in this period (to 1909) coincided with record profits. Unfortunately, this could not continue, and in failing to come to grips with the need for rate increases starting around 1909, the ICC abused the powers granted it to set maximum rates by the Hepburn Act (1906) and started the railroads on their downhill slide.

Summary

The 1906–1907 ICC investigation of the consolidation and combination of railroads was limited geographically and with regard to ownership. It was really only an investigation of the Harriman lines, and while it contained a strong flavor of concern about competition, a disproportionate part of the investigation was of the Chicago & Alton reorganization where such concerns were unimportant and in fact barely mentioned by the Commission itself. While it cannot be proved with certainty, a strong and plausible *prima facie* case can be made that the investigation was the result of the break between Harriman and Roosevelt. That break primarily resulted from Harriman's refusal to provide campaign money for the Republican party in 1906 and Roosevelt's reneging on an earlier promise to Harriman when his aid in raising funds was sought in 1904. Roosevelt's righteous indignation appears quite cynical in this instance. He was "playing to the balcony" to increase his chances in the next election. Harriman (and his reputation) was the innocent victim of political maneuvering and confused thinking.

While the government did pursue, and obtain, the dissolution of the *de facto* Union Pacific–Southern Pacific merger after the conclusion of the ICC investigation, no charges were forthcoming from the rather sensational investigation itself. It did create concern both on Wall Street and among railroad men that the government would pursue a similar course with regard to other systems. This did not occur, further supporting the belief that this investigation was essentially an attempt to "get" Harriman.

The Commission's case and analysis were faulty on almost every issue. The Commission missed important points that made the Union Pacific–Southern Pacific joint control reasonable and efficient regardless of the absolute statements of law and theory. Because the latter ruled in the courts, the government eventually won. The trial court dismissed the government's allegation that competition for transcontinental traffic had been restrained by the combination after finding no substantial competition between the two railroads. Then the Supreme Court reversed the lower court with the finding that substantial competition existed between the Union Pacific and the Southern Pacific before the combination. This primarily rested on the fact that both roads maintained soliciting offices in eastern cities. General condemnation of the economic power of the Harriman lines, rather than conviction that the two railroads had been competitors, appears to be the basis of the Supreme Court's reversal of the trial court's extensive findings that there was no substantial competition.

The investigation did not produce the results apparently desired by the regulators. It unfortunately did blacken one man's reputation in the eyes of the public. This was the regulator's reward for Edward Henry Harriman, the greatest railroad rebuilder and organizer of his (and probably any) age. It seems a poor reward from the public that shared in the fruits of his labor and genius: the significant improvement of the capacity and productivity of his railroads.

CHAPTER TEN

Lessons for the 1980s and Beyond

In his own time E. H. Harriman was recognized as a titan of the business world, and not only by the world of business but the world at large. The outcome of specific procedures and techniques and even the style Harriman employed in management and finance were so attractive that others soon emulated them and their source is now neither noted nor remembered. If one wanted success, one tried-and-proven route was to follow the successful. Few have been so successful as Harriman, nor so visible, especially during the period of his greatest powers, 1898–1909.

It is easy to see Harriman's significance for the American economy and business system of the pre–World War I era of the twentieth century. An interesting question, but a far harder one to answer, is whether he has significance for the business world and the American economy in this ninth decade of the twentieth century. It would be easy to say no. The story of Harriman's achievements is a glorious one for those seemingly far off days when the railroad was the supreme transportation mode and silicon chips were something one brushed off before entering the well-kept house. In the 1980s the railroad is still extremely important, but it is hardly supreme. Amtrak and Conrail are familiar names reflecting the failure of the railroads to survive under private auspices under the heavy burden of regulation since Harriman's heyday. It may be argued that genuine private control of the railroads ended within the decade following Harriman's death. What failed was the attempt to set transportation policy through a governmental commission which in the end was neither responsible nor responsive to demonstrated needs. Even massive taxpayer subsidies have failed to paper over the neglect and mistakes of the past.

We now are in the midst of a movement to deregulation that may succeed in restoring some sanity and improve the efficiency of our transportation system.

The railroad's loss of passenger traffic is a well-known story resulting from the success of innovations still in their infancy in Harriman's heyday: the internal combustion engine and the airplane. On the freight side of the ledger the story is more complex. Again the internal combustion engine played an important role. The trucking industry's natural inroads into the lifeblood of the railroads, the freight business, has unfortunately been amplified by the mismanagement of regulation by Harriman's old nemesis the Interstate Commerce Commission. The Commission's long history of favoring the trucking industry over the railroads in the name of cultivating "competition" has imposed significant costs on both the railroads and society over the last half century or more, and we are not done bearing these costs. With the move to deregulation there is now hope this too will end. An innovation that Harriman never even heard of, the computer ranks among the leading industries of our day. The silicon chip is no longer a trivial nuisance; it is both ubiquitous and extremely important. Business empires can rise or fall on the latest improvements in the lowly chip. All in all, the world is far changed from that where Harriman was acclaimed the "colossus of the railroads."

What then of the significance of Harriman and his career for society and the business world of the 1980s? The easy answer that there is no significance is based on outward appearances, on the superficial rather than the core of the matter. The answer that there *is* significance, which is the answer here, requires that we look more deeply than the obvious changes suggested. Where we must look is at the central core of business reality. This has changed far less than appearances indicate. In fact, in the matters that really count, it has changed little from Harriman's era. The bottom line is still to serve the public and to do so efficiently so as to earn (at least) the opportunity cost (what one can earn in the next best employment) of the resources one employs. Society, the owners of those resources, and the manager and financier all gain. This is precisely as it was in Harriman's day. The reason he was successful was that he did serve the public, and he did so efficiently. How he did this is what is significant for the 1980s. Harriman's accomplishments were an outgrowth of what we may call his business principles. Five major business principles are discernible in Harriman's activities.

First and foremost of Harriman's principles was that of putting the railroad in first-class physical condition. This derives from the classic requirement for business success—the need to be the low-cost producer, or one of them. Putting the railroad in first-class physical condition would improve its efficiency, i.e., reduce the cost of doing business per unit of output. That change would push profit up given the level of output. Probably more important, it would enable the railroad to serve its territory better and build goodwill among shippers and the traveling public. Improved conditions would make this possible not only for the given level of output, but also for rising levels of output coincident with business prosperity and economic growth. The outcome would be not only goodwill but a further rise in profits. Rising security prices and improved credit for the railroad would follow. We see the implementation of this principle with every railroad Harriman managed. While it is most obvious in the case of the Union Pacific and the Southern Pacific, putting the property in first-class physical shape was the first and major undertaking for every Harriman railroad. It was the essential cornerstone of his business philosophy. It was the major point behind Harriman's belief (and frequent statement) that, "The way to save money is to spend money."

The second principle was the other part of his basic credo and the corollary of the first. He believed maintenance of the property to be of cardinal importance. Not only must the property be put in first-class physical condition, but it must be kept in that condition. This does not happen by magic or inadvertence. It required a willingness to plough profits back into the business in very substantial amounts. Even Ripley, a strong detractor of Harriman, concedes what Harriman did in the matter of maintenance when he notes with regard to the Union Pacific and the Southern Pacific, "The fact that for years the expenditures annually for maintenance of way were often 50 per cent [sic] greater per mile than for other properties in the same territory is itself eloquent testimony to the thoroughness of the physical side of the work."[1] Ploughing back profits for maintenance was the correct course of action because Harriman believed that service to the public and shippers is the basis of the railroad's business and that service took precedence over dividends to stockholders. Along with physical improvement of the property, abundant maintenance is a hallmark of all of Harriman's railroads.

Putting the property in first-class physical condition and maintaining that state was fundamental to Harriman, but he correctly saw that this was only part of the battle. Emphasis on managerial competence and its reward was the other leg on which first-class service for the railroad's public must rest. Such competence was essential to obtaining an excellent product from first-class physical capital. Railroads don't run themselves, people run railroads. The quality of those people is an important input in the railroad's production process. It is often overlooked that the inherent superiority of the railroads, as with any precision device, depends upon capable, well-disciplined operation. Harriman demanded and got competent management. Beyond this, Harriman also saw correctly that managers aren't the only people input for the railroad. His principle of competence and reward extended to all levels of the organization. He realized that appropriate reward was essential for competent service down to the lowliest employee in the hierarchy. Happy employees are most likely to be good employees too. Harriman's railroads paid good wages and were also pioneers in pension plans, hospital and medical departments, educational work, and employees' clubs. His railroads were among the first, if not the first, to adopt a pension plan for railroad labor. Moreover, this was done some years before union demands for such benefits and the establishment of the federal retirement system for railroad workers. All of these actions reflected Harriman's third principle: the emphasis on competency and its reward.

Harriman's fourth principle was of special importance because it provided the means by which he could practice the others. This was that sound finance is the cornerstone for success. For Harriman this was an apt description. After joining the board of the Illinois Central in the 1880s, he became chairman of the executive committee and had the ultimate responsibility for Illinois Central finances. His satisfaction of this responsibility demonstrated great ability, resourcefulness, and farsightedness. The unique skill with which he managed the railroad's finances became apparent to others and played a role in providing the opportunity to manage the Union Pacific. What he learned and the connections he developed in the financial world were also a part of this development. Harriman's guidance of the Illinois Central's finances is well characterized by Otto Kahn's statement that for the Illinois Central, "Somehow or other, it never had bonds for sale except when bonds were in great demand; it never borrowed money except when money was cheap and abundant."[2]

Included in the principle of sound finance was the subsidiary principle of boldness and daring in borrowing. Bold use of credit was a characteristic of Harriman's financial policy. It is obvious that borrowing at low rates and using the funds to create capital that pays a higher rate is good business. However, the risks involved in heavy mortgage indebtedness operated as a deterrent to substantial borrowing. Still Harriman's firms borrowed freely. His spectacular success with the Union Pacific and the Southern Pacific owed much to the 1901 issue of $100 million in bonded debt by the Union Pacific. As we saw earlier, this seemingly huge increase in funded debt turned out in the end to be no increase at all. This resulted from the fact that the bonds were convertible to common stock, and the torrent of earnings unleashed by the rebuilding of the Union Pacific (and the effects of the ongoing economic upturn and growth of the West) made conversion so attractive that the debt completely disappeared. Thus, the railroad at one stroke obtained a sizable war chest for productive investment, was freed from the weight of mortgage debt thus incurred, and found its credit enormously strengthened for future borrowing. All of this was the result of bold borrowing, astutely structured: sound finance of the highest order.

Sound finance cannot operate in a vacuum. There is a market for funds and there are institutional agents who provide the operational framework for that market. Harriman had learned his lessons well on Wall Street. Borrowers are demanders of funds and demand and supply must get together in the market. A second subsidiary principle of Harriman's sound finance was the development of a financial base, a working relationship, with great institutions that could supply funds. For Harriman this principle was reflected in the close relationship he maintained throughout the height of his career with Kuhn, Loeb & Company and the National City Bank of New York. To a lesser extent he also relied on individuals and other institutions like the insurance companies. These relationships with the great suppliers of funds were the vital factor that made Harriman's sound finance work, and work very well indeed.

While differences of opinion can easily arise regarding their specific implementation, the four principles discussed are not the stuff of serious controversy. Such is not the case for the fifth of Harriman's business principles. This principle was the avoidance of what he viewed as destructive competition. In particular, he wanted no part in the bloodletting of the fierce rate wars with rates set below cost to which such competition too often descended. Harriman believed that rate wars of this kind resulted in practices that were not in the interests of either the railroads or the public. Those interests were far better served in Harriman's view by avoidance of such destructive competition and the maintenance of what he termed a "community of interest" among competing firms.

Naturally the suspicion arises that what Harriman was really after here was monopoly power. In fact, what he advocated and did (with the Union Pacific–Southern Pacific de facto merger) was to anticipate by twenty years the solution to the railroads' problems proposed in the Transportation Act of 1920 and Professor Ripley's consolidation plan. He wanted to reduce the number of competing railroads by regrouping them into a smaller number of consolidated, or cooperating, systems. He envisioned that these new organizations would be governed by the law. They would not be given free rein for monopoly.

On this issue Harriman was a prophet without honor. He was right, but persecuted for his views and actions in this regard. Later the regulatory agency that attacked him on these grounds itself propounded the same views and actions. The nation's two largest railroads in 1982 are just such consolidations: the Burlington Northern and the CSX System, approved if not fostered by the ICC. Recently a new consolidation was approved by the ICC creating the third largest railroad, and appropriately enough this consolidation includes the Union Pacific. On 13 September 1982 the ICC approved the merger of three profitable railroads: the Union Pacific, the Missouri Pacific, and the Western Pacific into a single new railroad, the Pacific Rail System. In what has been termed an unprecedented display of merger enthusiasm, the Union Pacific was allowed to buy the other two roads for upwards of $1 billion. Before the merger, the Union Pacific found itself with two western legs. One from Utah to the Pacific Northwest and another to Los Angeles (the Los Angeles & Salt Lake Railroad, formerly the San Pedro, Los Angeles & Salt Lake Railroad, purchased in 1921), both connected to the old main stem and its supporting lines ending in Omaha. The Western Pacific now provides what Harriman sought with the 1901 take-over of the Southern Pacific, a westward connection to the San Francisco Bay area. This, of course, reduced the Union Pacific's dependence (need to interchange traffic) on the Southern Pacific (the old Central Pacific). It is not much of a surprise that the Southern Pacific is appealing the merger to the courts. The other leg of the merger (the Missouri Pacific) gives the Union Pacific a midwestern and southern network that covers much of the territory included in the Illinois Central of Harriman's day. Through Nebraska and Colorado there is significant overlap between the former Union Pacific and the Missouri Pacific.

Here officially approved is exactly the system Harriman must have had in mind in 1901. In a de facto way he had it with control of the Union Pacific, the Southern Pacific, and the Illinois Central. He certainly did not have official approval, quite the reverse. Is the ICC concerned that this consolidation will reduce competition? No, it is not, although competing railroads, especially the Southern Pacific, are arguing strenuously that it does. It should be noted that the ICC included several stipulations in its approval aimed at easing any anticompetitive impact on the merger. As an example, several smaller railroads are guaranteed use of specific sections of the new railroad's track. The Southern Pacific is permitted to use certain Union Pacific tracks that could save it $100 million for upgrading parallel tracks. The statement of the ICC chairman on this merger is particularly illuminating (and somewhat amusing) because it is surely exactly the statement that Harriman would have made for such a consolidation. Reece Taylor (ICC chairman) said the new railroad "will enhance efficiency and competition while providing improved service to shippers." In addition he added that, "this consolidation represents another major step in the restructuring and revitalization of the nation's railroad system."[3] If Harriman's lead had been followed, such would have occurred decades ago and society would have enjoyed the efficiency gains for several decades. Now we have such restructuring occurring as a means of extricating us from the morass created by decades of regulatory neglect and misjudgments. Failure to follow Harriman earlier, compounded by another seven decades of mismanagement by the ICC, make restructuring and revitalization mandatory today.

The Pacific Rail System merger is still subject to legal challenge and such challenges are being undertaken. Harriman's difficulties were not with the ICC alone, but also with the courts. It will be interesting to see if the new merger survives the courts. The question now is, will the courts follow the ICC in accepting Harriman's wisdom on this issue? This turn of events would surely have been amusing to Harriman if he could have foreseen it. The fundamental problem here is that the responsibility is really that of Congress. As in many other areas, Congress is not meeting its responsibility and both the ICC and the courts are in a sense second-guessing Congress.

The merger movement of United States railroads continues with the 28 September 1983 announcemnt of the plan to merge the Southern Pacific Company and Santa Fe Industries, Inc. An attempt to merge these two roads was rejected by the ICC on anticompetitive grounds in 1980. Given recent developments, the new proposal stands a good chance of success. Merger of the Southern Pacific and Santa Fe would create a 25,600-mile rail system stretching from the Pacific Coast to Chicago, Kansas City, and New Orleans. The new system would be the third largest in mileage behind the Burlington Northern (28,900 miles) and the CSX (26,400 miles).

The Southern Pacific–Santa Fe merger completes creation of a United States rail system much like that Harriman envisioned. What remains to be settled is the status of Conrail, Illinois Central Gulf, and a few smaller regional lines like the Kansas City Southern Railroad.

Two major movements in the business, economic, and political spheres of the early 1980s are significant in relation to Harriman's career. The first of these is the deregulation effort begun by the federal government in the late 1970s with the Airline Deregulation Act of 1978 and the Motor Carrier Act of 1980. The rationale for this effort is the improvement of the economy's efficiency. This, as we have seen, was a major underlying aim of Harriman. He would certainly have applauded the deregulation movement especially as it applies to transportation: the airline and trucking industries. His own efforts for productivity improvement were attacked and to some extent undone by regulation. The federal government's recent efforts at deregulation represent a movement away from the political-economic mind set that was rising to power and full flower in Harriman's day. As such it is a movement toward the environment for which Harriman strove. Some aspects of the deregulation movement would not have pleased him. He was against cutthroat (below cost) competition. We have unfortunately seen a significant amount of this destructive competition in the wake of deregulation, and some of the victims, for example, Braniff, are now out of action. While in the short term they may have gained from such competition, it is by no means clear that the long run will be totally beneficial to consumers. Harriman would have argued for deregulation, but abstinence from destructive competition.

His belief in a "community of interest" and appropriate consolidation of firms might suggest that Harriman would also have applauded the second major movement in the business and economic spheres that has recently attracted so much attention. This is the seemingly ever-rising wave of business mergers (take-overs) in the American economy. It is not, in fact, so clear that these activities fit into the basic Harriman philosophy. His interest in consolidation was to improve efficiency and service. Other considerations appear to weigh more heavily in the gigantic mergers we see in the early 1980s. The profit attainable by the acquirer because of tax advantages or the liquidity position of acquired companies is frequently the apparent motive in these take-overs. Efficiency and service gains appear to occupy a secondary position. Of course, financial institutions and agents profit handsomely from the take-over efforts. Harriman was after all a financier as well as a manager. Perhaps his views of present-day merger activity would have been modified if he were contemplating it in his financier role.

The significance of Harriman's career and activities for the 1980s and beyond lies in the continued relevance of his basic business principles. The business person today who adopted these principles and carried them through would have the framework for success. Putting productive capacity in first-class shape, maintaining it in that condition, insisting on managerial (and worker) competence, using sound finance including bold borrowing and development of capital sources, and avoidance of destructive competition are keys to higher profit and better service to customers today just as they were eight decades ago when Harriman was in full swing. The political and social climates today are as amenable to the employment of these principles as they were in Harriman's day. In the end the real significance of Harriman for the 1980s and beyond is that if every business person followed Harriman's principles, efficiency and profits would rise and the consuming public would be better served. What better legacy can one businessman leave to later generations than a blueprint drawn from his beliefs and actions that points the way for improved welfare for society? As our study of his career and actions has shown, this is precisely what Edward Henry Harriman left us: a guideline for a better future.

NOTES AND REFERENCES

Chapter One

1. John Muir, *Edward Henry Harriman* (Garden City, N.Y.: Doubleday, Page & Company, 1912), 39.
2. Otto H. Kahn, *Edward Henry Harriman* (New York: C. G. Burgoyne, 1911), 34.
3. George Kennan, *E. H. Harriman: A Biography,* (Boston: Houghton Mifflin Company, 1922), 1:51.

Chapter Two

1. Bernard Baruch, *Baruch: My Own Story* (New York: Henry Holt & Company, 1957), 305.
2. Stuart Daggett, *Railroad Reorganization* (Boston: Houghton Mifflin Company, 1908), 260.
3. William Z. Ripley, *Railroads, Finance and Organization* (New York: D. Appleton & Company, 1920), 214.
4. Kennan, *E. H. Harriman,* 1:364.

Chapter Three

1. Kennan, *E. H. Harriman,* 1:74.
2. Ibid., 1:90.

Chapter Four

1. Lloyd J. Mercer, *Railroads and Land Grant Policy* (New York: Academic Press, 1982), 83, 86, 88, 91.

Chapter Five

1. Kennan, *E. H. Harriman,* 1:237.
2. E. H. Harriman, speech given at the opening of the St. Louis Exposition, 1 May 1904.

Chapter Six

1. Albro Martin, *James J. Hill and the Opening of the Northwest* (New York: Oxford University Press, 1976), 477.
2. Ibid., 488.
3. Joseph G. Pyle, *The Life of James J. Hill,* (Garden City, N.Y.: Doubleday, Page & Company, 1917), 2:141.
4. Carl Snyder, "Harriman: Colossus of Roads," *Review of Reviews* (January 1907).
5. Daggett, *Railroad Reorganization,* 260.
6. Kennan, *E. H. Harriman,* 2:79.
7. Ibid., 2:82.
8. Ripley, *Railroads,* 209.

Chapter Seven

1. Ripley, *Railroads,* 262.
2. George Kennan to Norman Firth, 27 August 1923, Kennan papers, Library of Congress.
3. Kennan, *E. H. Harriman,* 2:308.
4. Ibid., 2:241.

Chapter Eight

1. Daggett, *Railroad Reorganization,* 382–83.
2. Ripley, *Railroads,* 214, 405.
3. Daggett, *Railroad Reorganization,* 58.
4. Kennan, *E. H. Harriman,* 1:364.
5. "Studies in Operation—The Erie Railroad," *Railway Age Gazette,* 16 April 1916, pp. 939–42.
6. *Commercial & Financial Chronicle* (New York), 11 April 1908.
7. *Financial World* (New York), 3 September 1909.

Chapter Nine

1. Kennan, *E. H. Harriman,* 2:179.
2. Ibid., 2:200–201.
3. "In the Matter of Consolidations and Combinations of Carriers, Relations between Such Carriers, and Community of Interests Therein, Their Rates, Facilities and Practices," Interstate Commerce Commission, Reports, no. 943, vol. 12 (Washington, D. C.: Government Printing Office, 1908), 281.
4. Ibid., 302.
5. Ibid., 304–96.

Chapter Ten

1. Ripley, *Railroads*, 514.
2. Kahn, *Edward Henry Harriman*, 1.
3. *Los Angeles Times*, 14 September 1982, part 1, pp. 1, 9.

BIBLIOGRAPHICAL ESSAY

There are several general publications that the reader can profitably use to learn about Harriman's time period, what was happening to securities, how the railroads were doing, and tidbits about individuals including Harriman. The *Commercial and Financial Chronicle*, now available in microfilm, is a goldmine of information on the economy, securities, and the railroads. For information on specific railroads and the railroad system two sources provide a wealth of statistical data. These are the annual volumes of *Poor's Manual of the Railroads of the United States* (New York: Poor's Railroad Manual Company) and the annual volumes of the *Report on the Statistics of Railways in the United States*, Division of Statistics, Interstate Commerce Commission.

A source not to be overlooked for the period before radio and television is the general magazine. There were many of them and they covered everything of interest. The major magazines well worth reading include: *Cosmopolitan, Everyman, Harper's Weekly, Literary Digest, Review of Reviews*, and *World's Work*. In those days before television these were major sources of entertainment and information.

In the following, the specific sources used in this work, and available on Harriman, are discussed by chapter. This provides a road map for the reader and researcher interested in pursuing these issues further.

Chapter One

One major problem for the researcher working on E. H. Harriman is that there is no large body of Harriman's personal papers in existence. Some papers can be found at Arden Farms at Arden, New York. Another file exists at the Harriman offices at 63 Wall Street in New York City. The reason a substantial body of papers does not exist is said to be that the vast bulk of his personal papers was destroyed in the Equitable Building fire in 1912. Judge Lovett who became chairman of the Union Pacific Board after Harriman is apparently the original source of this information (letter to George Kennan while Kennan was working on the biography) and it has been passed down for the past seventy years. The author has discovered that this is not entirely correct. A considerable body of Harriman papers (including his letters from 1898 to 1909) did exist at Arden as of June 1921. At that time about 100 packages of Harriman papers were sent to storage at an unspecified garage. The present location (or existence) of most of these papers is not known although some of those sent to the garage at that time are now at Arden Farms. The only available body of Harriman letters is in the Archives of the Illinois Central Railroad at the Newberry Library in Chicago. Because of this paucity of personal papers the researcher is confined almost entirely to secondary sources in studying Harriman and his activities.

Two biographies on Harriman are available. The most thorough of these is *Edward Henry Harriman: A Biography* by George Kennan (Boston: Houghton Mifflin Company, 1922). This two-volume work covers all the major incidents in Harriman's life in considerable detail. While he started out with a bias against Harriman, George Kennan became a strong supporter of Harriman after his investigation of the Chicago & Alton reorganization. This shows through quite clearly in his writing. Kennan is somewhat limited in his characterization of Harriman. In particular, and surprising given his enthusiasm for Harriman, Kennan really doesn't provide us with a complete picture of the whole man as a human being. Kennan's letters (both those sent and received) are available in the Library of Congress. Reading the letters provides a considerable amount of information about the biography. In particular, the reason the Kennan biography lacks personal information about Harriman is because Mrs. Harriman suppressed such material. Not surprisingly, for a lady of her station and time, she considered personal details about Harriman "too intimate" for public discussion. The author has seen the suppressed pages and they do contain substantial personal information about Harriman and his activities. It is unfortunate that such information was not included in the biography.

In addition, Kennan wrote four other little books during the eight years he was working on the biography. These are interesting and contain some details not found in the biography, but in general the material of these books is included in the biography. The first book is *The Chicago & Alton Case: A Misunderstood Transaction* (Garden City, New York: Country Life Press, 1916). A part of this book first appeared in the *North American Review* of January 1916.

The second book is *Misrepresentation in Railroad Affairs* (Garden City, New York: Country Life Press, 1916). The book title is the title of chapter 1 in this book. Chapter 2 is entitled, "The Psychology of Mr. Roosevelt." This thirteen-page chapter is largely material that is not in the biography. It offers strong support for Kennan's charges against Roosevelt in the biography. Portions of this book also appeared in the *North American Review* of May and June 1916.

The third book is *E. H. Harriman's Far Eastern Plans* (Garden City, New York: Country Life Press, 1917). This book tells in detail of Harriman's trip with his family and advisors to the Far East in 1905 and of the ideas and plans that Harriman had for a round-the-world railway.

The fourth book is *The Salton Sea: An Account of Harriman's Fight With the Colorado River* (New York: Macmillan Company, 1917). This is a fascinating story of an important event in Harriman's career and a major public service which he performed. The little book has several photographs, illustrations, and a map, none of which appear in the biography. It is worth examining for that reason although the details included are virtually identical with the material of chapters 23 and 24 of the biography.

The second biography, *E. H. Harriman: The Little Giant of Wall Street* by H. J. Eckenrode and Pocohontas Wight Edmunds (New York: Greenberg Publisher, 1933) is less thorough in its coverage of Harriman and his career than Kennan's. However, it is far more thorough in characterization. Eckenrode and Edmunds provide the most detail available anywhere on Harriman's character and personal attributes. Given this focus, they also provide the most information on Harriman's family. One interesting mistake in Eckenrode and Edmunds is the incorrect listing of Harriman's birth year as 1849.

An excellent short sketch of Harriman's life and career is provided in "E. H. Harriman, the Financier and the Railroads" in *The Vital Few* by Jonathan Hughes (Boston: Houghton Mifflin Company, 1966). This is the best starting place for a detailed overview of Harriman.

With regard to the family, some additional information is provided on Mrs. E. H. Harriman and Harriman's daughter, Mary, in *Who Was Who in America*. The *New York Times* obituary on Mrs. Harriman (8 November 1932) and the front-page story in the *New York Times* on Mary's death (19 December 1934) also provide a few nuggets not elsewhere available.

Harriman the man is also illuminated by the short publications of two of his friends, Otto Kahn and John Muir, written soon after his death. *Edward Henry Harriman* by Otto Kahn (New York: C. G. Burgoyne, 1911) is the longer and more detailed of these pieces. This is also available (along with an important addendum from a later speech) in Otto Kahn's book (which is an interesting collection of his speeches) *Of Many Things* (New York: Boni & Liveright, 1926). Kahn's close personal relationship with Harriman results in a work that provides some otherwise unavailable pieces of information about the man and his career including the best description of Harriman's character. *Edward Henry Harriman* by John Muir (Garden City, New York: Doubleday, Page & Company, 1912) also contains a number of tidbits of information and characterization not available elsewhere. Harriman and Muir's relationship was apparently entirely personal without the major business component of the Harriman and Kahn relationship. This is good because it provides some glimpses of Harriman unencumbered by business affairs. At the same time the limited interaction of Harriman and Muir makes Muir's exposition relatively limited.

While not a biography, a series of articles by C. M. Keys which appeared in *World's Work* (vol. 13, 1906–07) ("Harriman: The Man in the Making, His Early Life and Start," pp. 8455–8464; "Harriman: Building of His Empire," pp. 8437–8552; "The Spinner of the Golden Webs," pp. 8651–8664; "Salvage of the Two Pacifics," pp. 8791–8803) is quite thorough in the discussion of Harriman's career to that point and in characterization of Harriman the man. If Kennan's work is perhaps a bit too pro-Harriman, Keys's is to some extent the reverse. Of course, it was written during the ICC investigation and the anti-Harriman feeling of that time. Whatever anti-Harriman bias one may detect in Keys's articles, they are a valuable supplement to the other works. In fact, one can discern that some later writers (e.g., Eckenrode and Edmunds) borrowed heavily from Keys.

In a similar vein to Keys's work is the excellent three-part series entitled "An Empire Builder: Edward Henry Harriman" by William Almon Wolff which appeared in the *Elks Magazine* of September, October, and November 1927. Wolff is more balanced than Keys in his writing.

Two books by John Moody: *The Railroad Builders* and *The Masters of Capital* (both New Haven: Yale University Press, 1920), each have a short chapter on Harriman. The shortness of these pieces severely limits their thoroughness. They are at best light sketches. However, there are some gems to be found in them. Moody's description of the Harriman-Schiff interview relative to the reorganization of the Union Pacific in *The Railroad Builders* is the best and most complete available. It is better than that provided in Kennan. The key point is that Harriman used Illinois Central credit to carry the day against Schiff. With the sound credit of the Illinois Central Harriman could obtain the funds necessary for the Union Pacific reorganization at 3 or 3½ percent versus the 4 to 5 percent Kuhn, Loeb & Company would have to pay to obtain the same funds.

In *The Masters of Capital* Moody has one interesting minor piece of personal information that is at variance with every other writing. He says that Harriman's job in 1862 as an office boy for DeWitt C. Hays on Wall Street was obtained by his father. Other writers don't actually say who got him the job, but it seems improbable that the unworldly Orlando Harriman with his strong opposition to Harriman going to work was the person.

One especially interesting episode in Harriman's life was the 1899 Alaska expedition. The new book *Looking Far North* by William H. Goetzman and Kay Sloan (New York: Viking Press, 1982) gives an excellent detailed exposition of this episode.

Two magazine articles by people who worked for Harriman also provide some insights about the man. The two articles are: "Three Business Giants for Whom I Worked" by Julius Kruttschknitt in *American Magazine* (November 1921) and "He Never Commended—Yet He Never Forgot Good Work" by Samuel Morse Felton in *System* (March 1923).

Specific points detailed in chapter 1 are derived from information regarding Harriman or particular incidents in more general works. Two that provided information are: *Railroad Reorganization* by Stuart Daggett (Boston: Houghton Mifflin Company, 1908) and *Railroads, Finance and Organization* by William Z. Ripley (New York: D. Appleton & Company, 1920).

Chapter Two

The sketch of Harriman's career relies heavily on the works already discussed with regard to chapter 1. The biographies by Kennan and by Eckenrode and Edmunds provide detailed discussions of Harriman's career. As noted above, Kennan's work is somewhat more thorough in these factual matters. The basic outline is contained in Eckenrode and Edmunds's work, but some details are missing. Eckenrode and Edmunds take what might be termed a light approach to their subject. This has benefits for the reader and researcher in terms of characterization, etc., but it results in the neglect of a lot of the details that, taken together, are important in painting the whole picture.

In terms of the career sketch, the articles by Keys in *World's Work* are helpful and, taken by itself, this work provides a good overall picture of Harriman's career as does the series in the *Elks Magazine* by Wolff. Keys doesn't provide any substantial details beyond what is found in Kennan. Since Kennan wrote fifteen years later this is not really surprising. Wolff also doesn't provide substantial detail beyond Kennan.

Specialized writings yield bits of information on the Harriman career that are lacking in the general works. The article by Thomas Warner Mitchell, "The Growth of the Union Pacific and Its Financial Operations," *Quarterly Journal of Economics* (August 1907) is an especially useful specialized work. Stuart Daggett in *Railroad Reorganization* sets out a wealth of information, some of which helps in fleshing out an overall view of the Harriman career. Edward S. Mead's classic work, *Corporate Finance* (New York: D. Appleton & Company, 1914), also serves up a few tidbits as does Ripley's *Railroads, Finance and Organization*. The ICC report, *Interstate Commerce Commission Reports*, vol. 12, November 1906–December 1907 (Washington, D. C.: U. S. Government Printing Office, 1908), on its 1906–07 investigation of the Harriman lines performs the same function.

Chapter Three

The best source for the story of the Illinois Central is *Main Line of Mid-America: The Story of the Illinois Central* by Carlton J. Corliss (New York:

Creative Age Press, 1950). Corliss gives a good general history of the Illinois Central with a great many details. Harriman, of course, plays a prominent role in Corliss's story over the appropriate chronological period. At the same time Harriman is not Corliss's focus. The result is that while the treatment of Harriman in this work is adequate and some information is provided that is not available elsewhere, the researcher on Harriman is disappointed by the slimness of the Harriman story. One would like a great many more details on his activities with the Illinois Central than Corliss provides. Given Harriman's importance at the Illinois Central for more than a quarter century, it does seem that Corliss should have had more.

Fortunately, some of the necessary detail on Harriman and the Illinois Central is set forth by the biographies, especially that of Kennan. Some problems are presented by the biographies' treatment of specific episodes. The best example of conflicting accounts concerns the 1906 ouster of Stuyvesant Fish from the presidency of the Illinois Central. Kennan offers a quite detailed story of the chronology of events leading up to the final clash and of the final struggle itself. Since he is, if anything, perhaps too pro-Harriman, one is left with some concern that the tale may be shaded. Eckenrode and Edmunds, writing fifteen years after Kennan, spin a quite different story. The actions of Fish stated by Kennan as the source of director discontent with Fish are lightly touched and dismissed by Eckenrode and Edmunds. Their account of this episode is pro-Fish. Fish comes through as the aggrieved party. The reason for this flavor is the light account (in fact, virtually non-account) of Fish's irregular transactions with Illinois Central money. This is puzzling since at the same time no effort is made to show that Kennan's detailed account is wrong. One is left with the impression that what Kennan writes is what did happen. But if this is the case, it is difficult to be pro-Fish and anti-Harriman with regard to this episode. It seems clear that Harriman went a long way to save his old friend, but that Fish continued his irregular actions in what appears to be an arrogant manner.

The data underlying the analysis of rates of return and output per mile are derived for the Illinois Central (and for all the railroads included in this study) from company reports in the annual volumes of Henry V. Poor, *Manual of the Railroads of the United States* (New York: H. V. and H. W. Poor) and the *Historical Statistics of the United States Since Colonial Times* (Washington, D. C.: U. S. Government Printing Office, 1974) produced by the Bureau of the Census, U. S. Department of Commerce. The company accounts and reports in Poor are a treasure mine of information for the researcher interested in historic issues with respect to U. S. railroads. These are not always complete and sometimes the year to year consistency is less than one desires. Lack of perfection aside, these are an invaluable data source. Much the same information can be found in *Report on the Statistics of the Railroads of the United States,* Interstate Commerce Commission.

Chapter Four

For the Union Pacific, the biographies again are a rich source of information. A particularly valuable work on the Union Pacific's financial history in the years immediately following the 1898 reorganization is the *Quarterly Journal of Economics* article by Thomas Warner Mitchell, "The Growth of the Union Pacific and Its Financial Operations." Mitchell's article provides a large volume of information on the Union Pacific's financial operations that is not put together in any other source. One might do as Mitchell did and dig some of this information out of company reports in Poor and the *Commercial and Financial Chronicle*. However, other parts of this story come from sources not readily available (and perhaps not available at all) to the modern researcher. Moreover, Mitchell has the whole thing already put together.

Since the Union Pacific is one of the railroads included, Daggett's *Railroad Reorganization* is another useful source, especially on the reorganization. Daggett presents a considerable amount of detailed information not available elsewhere.

An overall history of the Union Pacific down to 1920 is given in *History of the Union Pacific* by Nelson Trottman (New York: Ronald Press Company, 1923). About 100 pages of this book covers the reorganization and the E. H. Harriman era with the Union Pacific. The information on the reorganization period (1892–1898) is quite detailed. Much of it is contained in Daggett, but some information found here is not included in Daggett. The account in Trottman of the Union Pacific during the Harriman era is a fine supplement to the material in the biographies. A number of specific pieces of information found here are not in the biographies which have less detail on this one railroad.

A short chapter in Frank H. Spearman, *Strategy of Great Railroads* (New York: Charles Scribner's Sons, 1904) contains information on the Union Pacific, especially some details about the reconstruction of the Union Pacific not available elsewhere. The most recent history of the Union Pacific, *Union Pacific Country* by Robert G. Athearn (Chicago: Rand McNally & Company, 1971) essentially ends with the reorganization in 1898. The discussion of the reorganization period complements the other sources on this subject.

The Railroad Builders by John Moody as discussed above has a short chapter, "The Life Work of Edward H. Harriman," which in particular has the best account of how Harriman got into the Union Pacific reorganization. Since this is the key to Harriman's career, Moody's story is especially useful. The same tale is included in the chapter, "Harriman and Hill" in *The Masters of Capital* by John Moody. Both of the Moody books contain other details of Harriman's Union Pacific career some of which are not provided in the other sources or not brought out in the same way by other authors.

Chapter Five

The basic story of the purchase of control of the Southern Pacific, Harriman's reconstruction of the Southern Pacific, and the combined operation of the Southern Pacific and the Union Pacific is to be found in the biographies. For richness of detail George Kennan, *E. H. Harriman: A Biography* is by far the best source. Eckenrode and Edmunds cover the basic material but with far less attention to detail.

The best account of the purchase of control of the Southern Pacific is to be found in the *Quarterly Journal of Economics* article by Thomas Warner Mitchell. Stuart Daggett in *Railroad Reorganization* also covers this ground in his discussion of the Union Pacific.

Histories of the Southern Pacific Railroad are an additional source of information. Stuart Daggett in *Chapters on the History of the Southern Pacific* (New York: Ronald Press Company, 1922) covers the period of Harriman control adequately, but with fewer specifics than some of the other sources, most notably Kennan. The same is true of the other major Southern Pacific history, *Southern Pacific: The Roaring Story of a Fighting Railroad* by Neill C. Wilson and Frank J. Taylor (New York: McGraw-Hill Book Company, 1952).

Some capital stock and investment estimates used here for the Southern Pacific, and also for the Union Pacific, are from *Railroads and Railroad Land Grants: A Study in Government Intervention* by Lloyd J. Mercer (New York: Academic Press, 1982).

Chapter Six

This chapter deals with one of the most interesting (and profitable) episodes of Harriman's career. A wide variety of sources are available on the activities contained in this episode of high finance. The Harriman biographies (Kennan and Eckenrode and Edmunds) both give the basic story. As was the case with other issues, Kennan provides richer detail.

Various biographies of James J. Hill also tell the basic story and add some information from the Hill point of view that is missing or not dealt with in as much detail in the Harriman biographies. A particularly useful source here is *James J. Hill and the Opening of the Northwest* by Albro Martin (New York: Oxford University Press, 1976). Martin presents the story clearly with fine attention to appropriate detail. It is also helpful that he writes from Hill's viewpoint. The older biography (2 volumes) *The Life of James J. Hill* by Joseph G. Pyle (New York: Doubleday, Doran & Co., 1922) is also useful and contains some points not found elsewhere.

An interesting sidelight on John W. Gates's participation in the battle between Harriman and Morgan for control of the Northern Pacific is provided in Gates's biography, *Bet A Million: The Story of John W. Gates* by Lloyd Wendt and Herman Kogan (New York: Bobbs-Merrill Co., 1948).

A helpful source relative to the Burlington is *Burlington Route: A History of the Burlington Lines* by Richard C. Overton (New York: Alfred A. Knopf, 1965). Overton's work contains a significant amount of information specific to the Burlington that bears on the Harriman-Hill struggle over control of the Burlington.

The Northern Securities Company and the Northern Securities case are dealt with in some detail by all the general sources cited. In addition, Ripley in *Railroads, Organization and Finance* and Otto Kahn in *Edward H. Harriman* touch on this as well as the battles for control of the Burlington and the Northern Pacific. The most detailed general source on the Northern Securities case is *A History of the Northern Securities Case* by Balthasar Henry Meyer (Madison, Wis.: Bulletin of the University of Wisconsin, no. 142, 1906). Meyer's work is particularly valuable because it is the only work that delves into the legal issues in substantial detail.

Given the eminence of its author, an especially interesting work dealing with the issues of this chapter is the article, "Harriman: Colossus of Roads" in *Review of Reviews* (January 1907) by Carl Snyder. The chapter "Harriman and Hill" in *The Masters of Capital* by John Moody provides a thorough discussion of the Harriman-Hill conflict and its outcome.

Chapter Seven

Again the biographies are the fundamental source. Kennan gives the fullest detail on the Chicago & Alton affair. At least 10 percent of his two volumes are devoted to the Chicago & Alton. Kennan's purpose in this is a strong defense of Harriman's actions.

Ripley's *Railroads, Organization and Finance* has a quite long section on Harriman and the Chicago & Alton. Several bits of useful data are contained in *Railroad Capitalization* by James C. Bonbright (New York: AMS Press, 1969). This was originally published (1920) by Columbia University Press in the series, *Studies in History, Economics and Public Laws*. Edward S. Mead in *Corporate Finance* also comments on the Chicago & Alton incident. Spearman in *Strategy of Great Railroads* has a short chapter on the Chicago & Alton with considerable detail on its reconstruction.

A detailed discussion of the Harriman syndicate and the Chicago & Alton is contained in the Interstate Commerce Commission report, "The Consolidation and Combination of Carriers; Relations Between Carriers and Community of Interest Therein; Their Rates; Facilities and Practices" (*Interstate Commerce Commission Reports*, vol. 12 (Washington, D. C.: U. S. Government Printing

Office, 1908). The ICC conclusions in this matter are also presented in detail in this report of the 1906–07 investigation.

Chapter Eight

The biographies, particularly Kennan, once again provide the basic story with respect to these relatively minor involvements in the Kansas City Southern, the Baltimore & Ohio, and the Erie. Keys's articles in *World's Work* also cover these episodes. The material is somewhat scattered in the sources, i.e., not all in one chapter or section.

Stuart Daggett in *Railroad Reorganization*, Edward S. Mead in *Corporate Finance*, and William Z. Ripley in *Railroads, Organization and Finance* all provide bits and pieces of these activities. Albro Martin in *James J. Hill* (1976) also touches on these.

Details of Harriman's entrance into the reorganization of the Kansas City Southern are given in *Bet A Million: The Story of John W. Gates* by Lloyd Wendt and Herman Kogan.

Specific details regarding the Baltimore & Ohio and Harriman's connection with that railroad are found in *The Story of the Baltimore & Ohio Railroad*, vol. 2, by Edward Hungerford (New York: G. P. Putnam's Sons, 1928). This is the best source for the Baltimore & Ohio relationship since even Kennan is light on this matter. In a similar way *Men of Erie: A Story of Human Effort* by Edward Hungerford (New York: Random House, 1946) provides considerable detail both on the Erie and Harriman's relationship with the railroad. Kennan's account of Harriman's activities with the Erie is more complete since he gave more attention to the Erie than to the Baltimore & Ohio.

An article in *Railway Age Gazette* (28 April 1916), "Studies in Operation—the Erie Railroad," comments on Harriman's impact on the Erie.

Chapter Nine

Any account and analysis of the ICC 1906–07 investigation must start with the ICC report on that investigation cited earlier. The biographies, especially Kennan, provide a great amount of associated information not available in the ICC report itself. A major item here, not mentioned at all, of course, in the ICC report is the relationship between Harriman and Roosevelt, and the rift between them. Again, Kennan provides the most detailed view.

Albro Martin in *James J. Hill*, Edward S. Mead in *Corporate Finance*, and William Z. Ripley in *Railroads, Organization and Finance* all afford views and information on the ICC investigation.

Chapter Ten

No previous writer has dealt specifically with this issue. All the sources cited earlier provide general input and insight into this question without themselves undertaking this particular assessment. One source especially useful in suggesting an overall framework here is *Forty Years After: An Appreciation of the Genius of Edward Henry Harriman, 1848–1909* by Robert A. Lovett (New York: Newcomen Society in North America, 1949). This is an address given by Lovett to the Newcomen Society in New York in 1949. Lovett wishes to show why Harriman was a genius in his field and to highlight the qualities that set him apart from the other great railroad managers and financiers. This is very helpful in thinking about what Harriman and his career have to say to us in the 1980s. In the end these considerations are the single most important reason for study of Edward Henry Harriman and his career.

INDEX

ABOUT THE AUTHOR

Lloyd J. Mercer is professor of economics at the University of California, Santa Barbara, and has been on the faculty since 1966, serving as departmental chairman from 1974 to 1979. He received a Ph.D. in economics from the University of Washington in 1967. His primary teaching interests include economic history and microeconomics; his research specialties include applied microeconomics and econometrics. Professor Mercer is the author of *Railroads and Land Grant Policy,* articles on the economic history of the United States concerning public policy issues and the Great Depression, and articles and monographs on water resource economics.